Mometrix TEST PREPARATION

AEPA®

Economics (35) Secrets Study Guide

DEAR FUTURE EXAM SUCCESS STORY

First of all, **THANK YOU** for purchasing Mometrix study materials!

Second, congratulations! You are one of the few determined test-takers who are committed to doing whatever it takes to excel on your exam. **You have come to the right place.** We developed these study materials with one goal in mind: to deliver you the information you need in a format that's concise and easy to use.

In addition to optimizing your guide for the content of the test, we've outlined our recommended steps for breaking down the preparation process into small, attainable goals so you can make sure you stay on track.

We've also analyzed the entire test-taking process, identifying the most common pitfalls and showing how you can overcome them and be ready for any curveball the test throws you.

Standardized testing is one of the biggest obstacles on your road to success, which only increases the importance of doing well in the high-pressure, high-stakes environment of test day. Your results on this test could have a significant impact on your future, and this guide provides the information and practical advice to help you achieve your full potential on test day.

Your success is our success

We would love to hear from you! If you would like to share the story of your exam success or if you have any questions or comments in regard to our products, please contact us at **800-673-8175** or **support@mometrix.com**.

Thanks again for your business and we wish you continued success!

Sincerely,
The Mometrix Test Preparation Team

Printed in the United States of America

TABLE OF CONTENTS

Introduction

Thank you for purchasing this resource! You have made the choice to prepare yourself for a test that could have a huge impact on your future, and this guide is designed to help you be fully ready for test day. Obviously, it's important to have a solid understanding of the test material, but you also need to be prepared for the unique environment and stressors of the test, so that you can perform to the best of your abilities.

For this purpose, the first section that appears in this guide is the **Secret Keys**. We've devoted countless hours to meticulously researching what works and what doesn't, and we've boiled down our findings to the five most impactful steps you can take to improve your performance on the test. We start at the beginning with study planning and move through the preparation process, all the way to the testing strategies that will help you get the most out of what you know when you're finally sitting in front of the test.

We recommend that you start preparing for your test as far in advance as possible. However, if you've bought this guide as a last-minute study resource and only have a few days before your test, we recommend that you skip over the first two Secret Keys since they address a long-term study plan.

If you struggle with **test anxiety**, we strongly encourage you to check out our recommendations for how you can overcome it. Test anxiety is a formidable foe, but it can be beaten, and we want to make sure you have the tools you need to defeat it.

Secret Key #1 – Plan Big, Study Small

There's a lot riding on your performance. If you want to ace this test, you're going to need to keep your skills sharp and the material fresh in your mind. You need a plan that lets you review everything you need to know while still fitting in your schedule. We'll break this strategy down into three categories.

Information Organization

Start with the information you already have: the official test outline. From this, you can make a complete list of all the concepts you need to cover before the test. Organize these concepts into groups that can be studied together, and create a list of any related vocabulary you need to learn so you can brush up on any difficult terms. You'll want to keep this vocabulary list handy once you actually start studying since you may need to add to it along the way.

Time Management

Once you have your set of study concepts, decide how to spread them out over the time you have left before the test. Break your study plan into small, clear goals so you have a manageable task for each day and know exactly what you're doing. Then just focus on one small step at a time. When you manage your time this way, you don't need to spend hours at a time studying. Studying a small block of content for a short period each day helps you retain information better and avoid stressing over how much you have left to do. You can relax knowing that you have a plan to cover everything in time. In order for this strategy to be effective though, you have to start studying early and stick to your schedule. Avoid the exhaustion and futility that comes from last-minute cramming!

Study Environment

The environment you study in has a big impact on your learning. Studying in a coffee shop, while probably more enjoyable, is not likely to be as fruitful as studying in a quiet room. It's important to keep distractions to a minimum. You're only planning to study for a short block of time, so make the most of it. Don't pause to check your phone or get up to find a snack. It's also important to **avoid multitasking**. Research has consistently shown that multitasking will make your studying dramatically less effective. Your study area should also be comfortable and well-lit so you don't have the distraction of straining your eyes or sitting on an uncomfortable chair.

The time of day you study is also important. You want to be rested and alert. Don't wait until just before bedtime. Study when you'll be most likely to comprehend and remember. Even better, if you know what time of day your test will be, set that time aside for study. That way your brain will be used to working on that subject at that specific time and you'll have a better chance of recalling information.

Finally, it can be helpful to team up with others who are studying for the same test. Your actual studying should be done in as isolated an environment as possible, but the work of organizing the information and setting up the study plan can be divided up. In between study sessions, you can discuss with your teammates the concepts that you're all studying and quiz each other on the details. Just be sure that your teammates are as serious about the test as you are. If you find that your study time is being replaced with social time, you might need to find a new team.

Secret Key #2 – Make Your Studying Count

You're devoting a lot of time and effort to preparing for this test, so you want to be absolutely certain it will pay off. This means doing more than just reading the content and hoping you can remember it on test day. It's important to make every minute of study count. There are two main areas you can focus on to make your studying count.

Retention

It doesn't matter how much time you study if you can't remember the material. You need to make sure you are retaining the concepts. To check your retention of the information you're learning, try recalling it at later times with minimal prompting. Try carrying around flashcards and glance at one or two from time to time or ask a friend who's also studying for the test to quiz you.

To enhance your retention, look for ways to put the information into practice so that you can apply it rather than simply recalling it. If you're using the information in practical ways, it will be much easier to remember. Similarly, it helps to solidify a concept in your mind if you're not only reading it to yourself but also explaining it to someone else. Ask a friend to let you teach them about a concept you're a little shaky on (or speak aloud to an imaginary audience if necessary). As you try to summarize, define, give examples, and answer your friend's questions, you'll understand the concepts better and they will stay with you longer. Finally, step back for a big picture view and ask yourself how each piece of information fits with the whole subject. When you link the different concepts together and see them working together as a whole, it's easier to remember the individual components.

Finally, practice showing your work on any multi-step problems, even if you're just studying. Writing out each step you take to solve a problem will help solidify the process in your mind, and you'll be more likely to remember it during the test.

Modality

Modality simply refers to the means or method by which you study. Choosing a study modality that fits your own individual learning style is crucial. No two people learn best in exactly the same way, so it's important to know your strengths and use them to your advantage.

For example, if you learn best by visualization, focus on visualizing a concept in your mind and draw an image or a diagram. Try color-coding your notes, illustrating them, or creating symbols that will trigger your mind to recall a learned concept. If you learn best by hearing or discussing information, find a study partner who learns the same way or read aloud to yourself. Think about how to put the information in your own words. Imagine that you are giving a lecture on the topic and record yourself so you can listen to it later.

For any learning style, flashcards can be helpful. Organize the information so you can take advantage of spare moments to review. Underline key words or phrases. Use different colors for different categories. Mnemonic devices (such as creating a short list in which every item starts with the same letter) can also help with retention. Find what works best for you and use it to store the information in your mind most effectively and easily.

Secret Key #3 – Practice the Right Way

Your success on test day depends not only on how many hours you put into preparing, but also on whether you prepared the right way. It's good to check along the way to see if your studying is paying off. One of the most effective ways to do this is by taking practice tests to evaluate your progress. Practice tests are useful because they show exactly where you need to improve. Every time you take a practice test, pay special attention to these three groups of questions:

- The questions you got wrong
- The questions you had to guess on, even if you guessed right
- The questions you found difficult or slow to work through

This will show you exactly what your weak areas are, and where you need to devote more study time. Ask yourself why each of these questions gave you trouble. Was it because you didn't understand the material? Was it because you didn't remember the vocabulary? Do you need more repetitions on this type of question to build speed and confidence? Dig into those questions and figure out how you can strengthen your weak areas as you go back to review the material.

Additionally, many practice tests have a section explaining the answer choices. It can be tempting to read the explanation and think that you now have a good understanding of the concept. However, an explanation likely only covers part of the question's broader context. Even if the explanation makes perfect sense, **go back and investigate** every concept related to the question until you're positive you have a thorough understanding.

As you go along, keep in mind that the practice test is just that: practice. Memorizing these questions and answers will not be very helpful on the actual test because it is unlikely to have any of the same exact questions. If you only know the right answers to the sample questions, you won't be prepared for the real thing. **Study the concepts** until you understand them fully, and then you'll be able to answer any question that shows up on the test.

It's important to wait on the practice tests until you're ready. If you take a test on your first day of study, you may be overwhelmed by the amount of material covered and how much you need to learn. Work up to it gradually.

On test day, you'll need to be prepared for answering questions, managing your time, and using the test-taking strategies you've learned. It's a lot to balance, like a mental marathon that will have a big impact on your future. Like training for a marathon, you'll need to start slowly and work your way up. When test day arrives, you'll be ready.

Start with the strategies you've read in the first two Secret Keys—plan your course and study in the way that works best for you. If you have time, consider using multiple study resources to get different approaches to the same concepts. It can be helpful to see difficult concepts from more than one angle. Then find a good source for practice tests. Many times, the test website will suggest potential study resources or provide sample tests.

Practice Test Strategy

If you're able to find at least three practice tests, we recommend this strategy:

UNTIMED AND OPEN-BOOK PRACTICE

Take the first test with no time constraints and with your notes and study guide handy. Take your time and focus on applying the strategies you've learned.

TIMED AND OPEN-BOOK PRACTICE

Take the second practice test open-book as well, but set a timer and practice pacing yourself to finish in time.

TIMED AND CLOSED-BOOK PRACTICE

Take any other practice tests as if it were test day. Set a timer and put away your study materials. Sit at a table or desk in a quiet room, imagine yourself at the testing center, and answer questions as quickly and accurately as possible.

Keep repeating timed and closed-book tests on a regular basis until you run out of practice tests or it's time for the actual test. Your mind will be ready for the schedule and stress of test day, and you'll be able to focus on recalling the material you've learned.

Secret Key #4 – Pace Yourself

Once you're fully prepared for the material on the test, your biggest challenge on test day will be managing your time. Just knowing that the clock is ticking can make you panic even if you have plenty of time left. Work on pacing yourself so you can build confidence against the time constraints of the exam. Pacing is a difficult skill to master, especially in a high-pressure environment, so **practice is vital**.

Set time expectations for your pace based on how much time is available. For example, if a section has 60 questions and the time limit is 30 minutes, you know you have to average 30 seconds or less per question in order to answer them all. Although 30 seconds is the hard limit, set 25 seconds per question as your goal, so you reserve extra time to spend on harder questions. When you budget extra time for the harder questions, you no longer have any reason to stress when those questions take longer to answer.

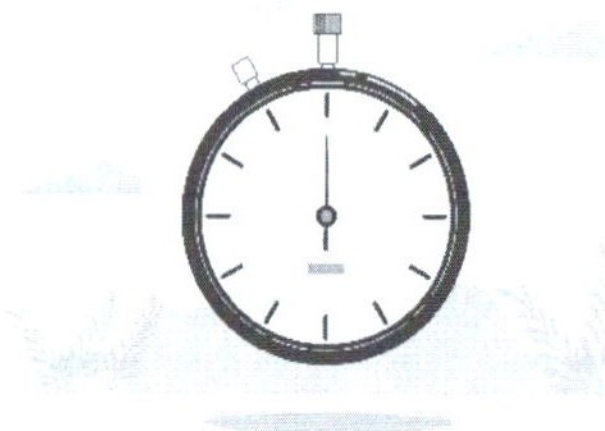

Don't let this time expectation distract you from working through the test at a calm, steady pace, but keep it in mind so you don't spend too much time on any one question. Recognize that taking extra time on one question you don't understand may keep you from answering two that you do understand later in the test. If your time limit for a question is up and you're still not sure of the answer, mark it and move on, and come back to it later if the time and the test format allow. If the testing format doesn't allow you to return to earlier questions, just make an educated guess; then put it out of your mind and move on.

On the easier questions, be careful not to rush. It may seem wise to hurry through them so you have more time for the challenging ones, but it's not worth missing one if you know the concept and just didn't take the time to read the question fully. Work efficiently but make sure you understand the question and have looked at all of the answer choices, since more than one may seem right at first.

Even if you're paying attention to the time, you may find yourself a little behind at some point. You should speed up to get back on track, but do so wisely. Don't panic; just take a few seconds less on each question until you're caught up. Don't guess without thinking, but do look through the answer choices and eliminate any you know are wrong. If you can get down to two choices, it is often worthwhile to guess from those. Once you've chosen an answer, move on and don't dwell on any that you skipped or had to hurry through. If a question was taking too long, chances are it was one of the harder ones, so you weren't as likely to get it right anyway.

On the other hand, if you find yourself getting ahead of schedule, it may be beneficial to slow down a little. The more quickly you work, the more likely you are to make a careless mistake that will affect your score. You've budgeted time for each question, so don't be afraid to spend that time. Practice an efficient but careful pace to get the most out of the time you have.

Secret Key #5 – Have a Plan for Guessing

When you're taking the test, you may find yourself stuck on a question. Some of the answer choices seem better than others, but you don't see the one answer choice that is obviously correct. What do you do?

The scenario described above is very common, yet most test takers have not effectively prepared for it. Developing and practicing a plan for guessing may be one of the single most effective uses of your time as you get ready for the exam.

In developing your plan for guessing, there are three questions to address:

- When should you start the guessing process?
- How should you narrow down the choices?
- Which answer should you choose?

When to Start the Guessing Process

Unless your plan for guessing is to select C every time (which, despite its merits, is not what we recommend), you need to leave yourself enough time to apply your answer elimination strategies. Since you have a limited amount of time for each question, that means that if you're going to give yourself the best shot at guessing correctly, you have to decide quickly whether or not you will guess.

Of course, the best-case scenario is that you don't have to guess at all, so first, see if you can answer the question based on your knowledge of the subject and basic reasoning skills. Focus on the key words in the question and try to jog your memory of related topics. Give yourself a chance to bring the knowledge to mind, but once you realize that you don't have (or you can't access) the knowledge you need to answer the question, it's time to start the guessing process.

It's almost always better to start the guessing process too early than too late. It only takes a few seconds to remember something and answer the question from knowledge. Carefully eliminating wrong answer choices takes longer. Plus, going through the process of eliminating answer choices can actually help jog your memory.

Summary: Start the guessing process as soon as you decide that you can't answer the question based on your knowledge.

How to Narrow Down the Choices

The next chapter in this book (**Test-Taking Strategies**) includes a wide range of strategies for how to approach questions and how to look for answer choices to eliminate. You will definitely want to read those carefully, practice them, and figure out which ones work best for you. Here though, we're going to address a mindset rather than a particular strategy.

Your odds of guessing an answer correctly depend on how many options you are choosing from.

Number of options left	5	4	3	2	1
Odds of guessing correctly	20%	25%	33%	50%	100%

You can see from this chart just how valuable it is to be able to eliminate incorrect answers and make an educated guess, but there are two things that many test takers do that cause them to miss out on the benefits of guessing:

- Accidentally eliminating the correct answer
- Selecting an answer based on an impression

We'll look at the first one here, and the second one in the next section.

To avoid accidentally eliminating the correct answer, we recommend a thought exercise called **the $5 challenge**. In this challenge, you only eliminate an answer choice from contention if you are willing to bet $5 on it being wrong. Why $5? Five dollars is a small but not insignificant amount of money. It's an amount you could afford to lose but wouldn't want to throw away. And while losing $5 once might not hurt too much, doing it twenty times will set you back $100. In the same way, each small decision you make—eliminating a choice here, guessing on a question there—won't by itself impact your score very much, but when you put them all together, they can make a big difference. By holding each answer choice elimination decision to a higher standard, you can reduce the risk of accidentally eliminating the correct answer.

The $5 challenge can also be applied in a positive sense: If you are willing to bet $5 that an answer choice *is* correct, go ahead and mark it as correct.

Summary: Only eliminate an answer choice if you are willing to bet $5 that it is wrong.

Which Answer to Choose

You're taking the test. You've run into a hard question and decided you'll have to guess. You've eliminated all the answer choices you're willing to bet $5 on. Now you have to pick an answer. Why do we even need to talk about this? Why can't you just pick whichever one you feel like when the time comes?

The answer to these questions is that if you don't come into the test with a plan, you'll rely on your impression to select an answer choice, and if you do that, you risk falling into a trap. The test writers know that everyone who takes their test will be guessing on some of the questions, so they intentionally write wrong answer choices to seem plausible. You still have to pick an answer though, and if the wrong answer choices are designed to look right, how can you ever be sure that you're not falling for their trap? The best solution we've found to this dilemma is to take the decision out of your hands entirely. Here is the process we recommend:

Once you've eliminated any choices that you are confident (willing to bet $5) are wrong, select the first remaining choice as your answer.

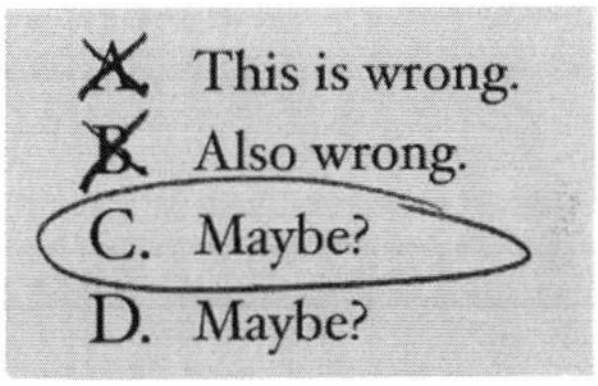

Whether you choose to select the first remaining choice, the second, or the last, the important thing is that you use some preselected standard. Using this approach guarantees that you will not be enticed into selecting an answer choice that looks right, because you are not basing your decision on how the answer choices look.

This is not meant to make you question your knowledge. Instead, it is to help you recognize the difference between your knowledge and your impressions. There's a huge difference between thinking an answer is right because of what you know, and thinking an answer is right because it looks or sounds like it should be right.

Summary: To ensure that your selection is appropriately random, make a predetermined selection from among all answer choices you have not eliminated.

Test-Taking Strategies

This section contains a list of test-taking strategies that you may find helpful as you work through the test. By taking what you know and applying logical thought, you can maximize your chances of answering any question correctly!

It is very important to realize that every question is different and every person is different: no single strategy will work on every question, and no single strategy will work for every person. That's why we've included all of them here, so you can try them out and determine which ones work best for different types of questions and which ones work best for you.

Question Strategies

✓ Read Carefully

Read the question and the answer choices carefully. Don't miss the question because you misread the terms. You have plenty of time to read each question thoroughly and make sure you understand what is being asked. Yet a happy medium must be attained, so don't waste too much time. You must read carefully and efficiently.

✓ Contextual Clues

Look for contextual clues. If the question includes a word you are not familiar with, look at the immediate context for some indication of what the word might mean. Contextual clues can often give you all the information you need to decipher the meaning of an unfamiliar word. Even if you can't determine the meaning, you may be able to narrow down the possibilities enough to make a solid guess at the answer to the question.

✓ Prefixes

If you're having trouble with a word in the question or answer choices, try dissecting it. Take advantage of every clue that the word might include. Prefixes can be a huge help. Usually, they allow you to determine a basic meaning. *Pre-* means before, *post-* means after, *pro-* is positive, *de-* is negative. From prefixes, you can get an idea of the general meaning of the word and try to put it into context.

✓ Hedge Words

Watch out for critical hedge words, such as *likely, may, can, often, almost, mostly, usually, generally, rarely,* and *sometimes.* Question writers insert these hedge phrases to cover every possibility. Often an answer choice will be wrong simply because it leaves no room for exception. Be on guard for answer choices that have definitive words such as *exactly* and *always.*

✓ Switchback Words

Stay alert for *switchbacks.* These are the words and phrases frequently used to alert you to shifts in thought. The most common switchback words are *but, although,* and *however.* Others include *nevertheless, on the other hand, even though, while, in spite of, despite,* and *regardless of.* Switchback words are important to catch because they can change the direction of the question or an answer choice.

⊘ Face Value

When in doubt, use common sense. Accept the situation in the problem at face value. Don't read too much into it. These problems will not require you to make wild assumptions. If you have to go beyond creativity and warp time or space in order to have an answer choice fit the question, then you should move on and consider the other answer choices. These are normal problems rooted in reality. The applicable relationship or explanation may not be readily apparent, but it is there for you to figure out. Use your common sense to interpret anything that isn't clear.

Answer Choice Strategies

⊘ Answer Selection

The most thorough way to pick an answer choice is to identify and eliminate wrong answers until only one is left, then confirm it is the correct answer. Sometimes an answer choice may immediately seem right, but be careful. The test writers will usually put more than one reasonable answer choice on each question, so take a second to read all of them and make sure that the other choices are not equally obvious. As long as you have time left, it is better to read every answer choice than to pick the first one that looks right without checking the others.

⊘ Answer Choice Families

An answer choice family consists of two (in rare cases, three) answer choices that are very similar in construction and cannot all be true at the same time. If you see two answer choices that are direct opposites or parallels, one of them is usually the correct answer. For instance, if one answer choice says that quantity x increases and another either says that quantity x decreases (opposite) or says that quantity y increases (parallel), then those answer choices would fall into the same family. An answer choice that doesn't match the construction of the answer choice family is more likely to be incorrect. Most questions will not have answer choice families, but when they do appear, you should be prepared to recognize them.

⊘ Eliminate Answers

Eliminate answer choices as soon as you realize they are wrong, but make sure you consider all possibilities. If you are eliminating answer choices and realize that the last one you are left with is also wrong, don't panic. Start over and consider each choice again. There may be something you missed the first time that you will realize on the second pass.

⊘ Avoid Fact Traps

Don't be distracted by an answer choice that is factually true but doesn't answer the question. You are looking for the choice that answers the question. Stay focused on what the question is asking for so you don't accidentally pick an answer that is true but incorrect. Always go back to the question and make sure the answer choice you've selected actually answers the question and is not merely a true statement.

⊘ Extreme Statements

In general, you should avoid answers that put forth extreme actions as standard practice or proclaim controversial ideas as established fact. An answer choice that states the "process should be used in certain situations, if..." is much more likely to be correct than one that states the "process should be discontinued completely." The first is a calm rational statement and doesn't even make a definitive, uncompromising stance, using a hedge word *if* to provide wiggle room, whereas the second choice is far more extreme.

⊘ Benchmark

As you read through the answer choices and you come across one that seems to answer the question well, mentally select that answer choice. This is not your final answer, but it's the one that will help you evaluate the other answer choices. The one that you selected is your benchmark or standard for judging each of the other answer choices. Every other answer choice must be compared to your benchmark. That choice is correct until proven otherwise by another answer choice beating it. If you find a better answer, then that one becomes your new benchmark. Once you've decided that no other choice answers the question as well as your benchmark, you have your final answer.

⊘ Predict the Answer

Before you even start looking at the answer choices, it is often best to try to predict the answer. When you come up with the answer on your own, it is easier to avoid distractions and traps because you will know exactly what to look for. The right answer choice is unlikely to be word-for-word what you came up with, but it should be a close match. Even if you are confident that you have the right answer, you should still take the time to read each option before moving on.

General Strategies

⊘ Tough Questions

If you are stumped on a problem or it appears too hard or too difficult, don't waste time. Move on! Remember though, if you can quickly check for obviously incorrect answer choices, your chances of guessing correctly are greatly improved. Before you completely give up, at least try to knock out a couple of possible answers. Eliminate what you can and then guess at the remaining answer choices before moving on.

⊘ Check Your Work

Since you will probably not know every term listed and the answer to every question, it is important that you get credit for the ones that you do know. Don't miss any questions through careless mistakes. If at all possible, try to take a second to look back over your answer selection and make sure you've selected the correct answer choice and haven't made a costly careless mistake (such as marking an answer choice that you didn't mean to mark). This quick double check should more than pay for itself in caught mistakes for the time it costs.

⊘ Pace Yourself

It's easy to be overwhelmed when you're looking at a page full of questions; your mind is confused and full of random thoughts, and the clock is ticking down faster than you would like. Calm down and maintain the pace that you have set for yourself. Especially as you get down to the last few minutes of the test, don't let the small numbers on the clock make you panic. As long as you are on track by monitoring your pace, you are guaranteed to have time for each question.

⊘ Don't Rush

It is very easy to make errors when you are in a hurry. Maintaining a fast pace in answering questions is pointless if it makes you miss questions that you would have gotten right otherwise. Test writers like to include distracting information and wrong answers that seem right. Taking a little extra time to avoid careless mistakes can make all the difference in your test score. Find a pace that allows you to be confident in the answers that you select.

⊘ Keep Moving

Panicking will not help you pass the test, so do your best to stay calm and keep moving. Taking deep breaths and going through the answer elimination steps you practiced can help to break through a stress barrier and keep your pace.

Final Notes

The combination of a solid foundation of content knowledge and the confidence that comes from practicing your plan for applying that knowledge is the key to maximizing your performance on test day. As your foundation of content knowledge is built up and strengthened, you'll find that the strategies included in this chapter become more and more effective in helping you quickly sift through the distractions and traps of the test to isolate the correct answer.

Now that you're preparing to move forward into the test content chapters of this book, be sure to keep your goal in mind. As you read, think about how you will be able to apply this information on the test. If you've already seen sample questions for the test and you have an idea of the question format and style, try to come up with questions of your own that you can answer based on what you're reading. This will give you valuable practice applying your knowledge in the same ways you can expect to on test day.

Good luck and good studying!

Basic Economic Concepts and Microeconomics

Introduction to Economics

Capital

Capital is a comprehensive term for all or any methods by which products are made by labor. This includes a wide variety of tools or elements. **Physical capital** may include all categories of real objects such as equipment, plants, land, and machinery that contribute to the process of production. **Intellectual capital** is the necessary ingredient that transforms the production process by human interaction. Included in intellectual capital is the utilization of information, management skills, and technological advances, as well as the application of ideas and theories which are catalysts in the economic system.

Although capital is generally regarded as an essential ingredient of benign economic activity, it can also be used to foster the **defense** of a state or prepare a country for an aggressive war. Large portions of Germany's capital were used by the Nazis in their attempt to dominate Europe. Capital is commonly used to further a state's **geopolitical aims** through peaceful or belligerent goals. The utilization of capital is a prime indicator of any country's goals and ambitions.

Historically, capital was considered to be physical equipment, machinery, plants, and other major investments used in manufacturing. The more modern concept of capital broadens the definition to include a wide range of **assets** that are utilized in the production process.

Financial capitalrepresents the operating funds and monetary investment in a business or plant. Financial capital is often obtained by corporations through the issue of stock in exchange for funds. Natural resources such as oceans, forests, mountains, and rivers provide **natural capital** which may or may not be publicly owned. Capital that is used to provide support systems for fundamental production processes and operating ability is sometimes termed **infrastructural capital**. Much of this type of capital is represented in plants and equipment. The abilities and acumen gained from education and experience are sometimes referred to as **human capital**. This incorporates the many types of growth and development from what we call human resources.

Factors of Production

Resources that are used in the production and manufacture of goods and services are called **factors of production**. They include land and natural products derived from land, including dirt, gems, minerals, and fodder. The cost of using land is usually rent in one form or another. Labor is another factor of production, and this is a blanket term for all individuals involved in the manufacturing, marketing, and transfer of goods and services. The payment for labor is designated as wages. Capital is the third essential factor of production. These definitions of the factors of production are from classical economics and political economy, and they remain accurate today, although the idea of capital has been expanded to include human expertise and technology.

Foundation of Economics as a Science

The study of economics includes **microeconomics**, which is concerned with smaller units, such as individuals and firms, and **macroeconomics**, which looks at the economy as a composite, taking a more global view. In general, economics deals with topics such as scarcity, supply, demand, and choices made by various parts of the economy and the total economy. There are a variety of economic topics that overlap both microeconomics and macroeconomics. These hybrid areas may be covered separately or as a part of the micro/macroeconomic spectrum. "Mainstream" economics is a blend of macroeconomics and economic theory developed in the last 50 years. This includes a number of schools of economic thought, each with its own assumptions, conclusions, and methodology. Economics centers on the idea of scarce resources and how to best utilize these resources to meet the needs of individuals and the economic system as a whole.

Mechanism Where the Study of Economics Occurs

The exchange of services and goods in an organized marketplace, where sellers and buyers vie to optimize their results by trading, is the **mechanism where the study of economics occurs**. Factors of production, the directed use of labor and capital, and the achievement of profit are the driving forces of an economic system. The clearest representation of these elements occurs in a **free market economy**, of which capitalism is the prime example. These factors are also in play in **state-controlled systems**, which include communism and socialism. Many contend that in all economic systems, the driving force is self-interest, or the "Invisible Hand" that Adam Smith defined in his Wealth of Nations. Economics may be studied in a wide spectrum of political, social, and financial systems. Commonalities and contrasts may be used as a method of comparing economic theory in a variety of settings. Many of the crucial components of economics are active in any organized society, regardless of its philosophy.

Beginnings of Economics as a Science

Political economy was defined as the economics of **competing states**, and was the term used by early economic thinkers. Neoclassical economists discarded this term in the late 1800s in favor of simply *economics*. The origin of the term *economics* is from the Greek word *oikonomikos*, meaning settlement laws. Economics was a recognized field in early Greek, Arab, and Roman eras. This is known as the **premodern period**. The mercantile and physiocrat systems are termed **early modern**, and what we now call economics is named **modern economics** in the history of economic thought. The pioneers of modern economic thought include such giants as Karl Marx, David Ricardo, John Stuart Mill, and of course, Adam Smith. Economic references and problems are discussed in early texts such as the Old and New Testaments. Economic thought has often played an important part in political systems such as Communism and Socialism and has played a major role in all societies.

Foundation of Modern Economics

Modern economics is based on one basic premise: that **resources** are scarce and limited, and that **choices** must be made in the acquisition and use of them. All other questions and alternatives flow from this assumption. Economic choices involve sacrificing something in order to obtain another thing. This sacrifice is called the "**opportunity cost**" of the choice. You may choose to spend your last dollar on a candy bar rather than a writing tablet, thus the opportunity cost of the candy bar is the tablet. There are seemingly endless choices in a consumer society, all of which involve choices and opportunity costs. The choices and opportunity costs are expressed in price relationships in modern economics. Each individual makes many economic decisions (choices) each day, and the aggregate reflects the economic activity of a society. Choices are driven by the **utility**, or want-satisfying abilities of the goods and services. Choices are ranked on the ability of the good or service to fill a perceived need of the individual. This utility function is active in most, but not all, economic choices.

Scarcity and Choice

Economics could rightfully be called the study of **scarcity**. Limited resources are available to satisfy the wants and needs of both individuals and states. Economics involves the **choices** made by an economy to satisfy these wants and needs. Every economy must choose what goods and services to produce, how to produce them, and for whom they are intended. Limitations of the factors of production—land, labor, and capital—sometimes make these choices difficult. When an economic choice is made, there is an "**opportunity cost**" implicit in the choice. The opportunity cost is what is given up by making a choice. If a country chooses to manufacture automobiles, it may not have the industrial capacity to produce tanks or aircraft. Thus, the economic choice to make automobiles involves the opportunity cost of not making tanks or aircraft. Individuals and countries continually make economic choices and sacrifice opportunist costs in the process. An individual may choose to attend a film rather than go out to dinner. Choices are driven by what people and countries feel is in their best interest.

Specialization and Division of Labor

Labor, a major factor of production, must be used in the most efficient manner to optimize the economic system. The concept of **specialization** requires that labor (and other factors of production) be used on work on which they are most efficient in order to produce goods in the most cost-effective manner. This means allocating specialized operations to various members of the workforce so each can concentrate on what he or she does best. The result should be an increase in productivity with a corresponding increased profitability of the firm. When this concept is extrapolated throughout an economy, it provides a country with a competitive advantage, that is to say, a nation, company, or individual will be producing most efficiently, giving a boost to productivity. Such an economy will tend to have an edge in international trade, and function more efficiently in the domestic economy.

Market Economy

A market economy is an economic system in which the **individuals** own and operate all factors related to production. It relies on **entrepreneurship** to spur markets for operation. The goal of individuals in a market economy is to obtain a profit from their chosen area of business. It is often associated with capitalism and private ownership of capital. Market economies are successful in part due to increased individual freedom for their members. When people have the freedom to make their own decisions, the economy is more likely to function efficiently. This is because changes in the markets will be noticed and responded to quickly and appropriately. There is more flexibility for economic action in a market economy system. Through private ownership and individual freedom, market economies are the most successful systems for the operations of free markets in the world. The largest market economies today are the United States, China, and Japan.

Review Video: Basics of Market Economy
Visit mometrix.com/academy and enter code: 791556

Economics in the Premodern Age

Ibn Khaldun of Tunis, writing in the 12th century, discussed political and economic theory. A favorite subject of his was population density and its effect on economic cycles. This is one of the earliest records of economic theory. **Scholasticism**, a theological school of philosophy in the Middle Ages, incorporated a debate over a number of basic economic issues, including how a fair price of something could be determined. In the wars between the Church and her reformers during the **Reformation**, the concept of free trade arose and was considered in both theological and political contexts. The church and nobility saw economic activity as a way to raise revenues, and imposed taxes on almost all transactions. These taxes were used to finance wars and enrich the ruling classes, almost never benefiting those being taxed. **Feudalism** imposed its own system of economics, determining how most economic affairs would be conducted and taxed. Needless to say, the serfs rarely saw any good from these measures.

Early Stirrings of Economic Thought

The **Mercantilists**, a group of European importers and exporters, strove to profit from exploring new markets, trading goods at a profitable rate, and growing their markets. Mercantilists were the dominant economic force in the new nation-states of Europe. Their activities were instrumental in leading to the discovery and settlement of the New World. The **Physiocrats**, a school of eco-philosophy active in France during the Enlightenment, were led by writers such as Anne Turgot and Francois Quesnay. Arguably, this was the first school or movement that viewed economics as a field in its own right. Many believe that modern economics was founded by the Physiocrats. Later thinkers and writers such as Adam Smith and David Ricardo built their theories on the foundation laid by the Physiocrats. As a group, the Physiocrats were short-lived, but their impact was significant in the development of economic thought.

Timeline of Economic Schools of Thought Through the Centuries

Schools of economic thought may be loosely categorized as follows:

- **16th-18th Century** - Dominated by the European nation-states who pioneered Mercantilism in an effort to enrich themselves through trade and exploration of new markets. The Physiocrats were an important 18th-century economic school that originated in France.
- **18th-19th Century** - Great economic thinkers and philosophers such as Adam Smith, John Stuart Mill, Thomas Malthus, and David Ricardo wrote important works that provided the foundation for Classical economics. This period also saw the rise of the "Utopian Socialists," who formulated economic ideas to cure the ills of society. Marxism is also included in this period, although it mixes political, social, and economic theory in a hybrid philosophy.
- **Late 19th Century** - Alfred Marshall is felt to be the father of Neoclassical economics. Marshall authored the concept of "marginal theory of value," which is the cornerstone of neoclassical economics.
- **20th Century** - Carl Menger wrote the seminal work on economics for what was to be called the Austrian school. The American Institutionalist school and German school of economics appeared during this period.

Principle of Comparative Advantage

Why would two countries continue to trade if one can produce goods and services cheaper than another? The answer is a **comparative advantage**, which depends upon the ratio between the costs of producing different products. This concept was introduced by **David Ricardo** in his seminal work on political economy and trade. Essentially, the principle states that each nation should specialize in producing the commodity with the lower opportunity cost. This would give the country a comparative advantage in exporting that product. It should trade with another country for a product for which it has a comparative disadvantage. Thus, each country will benefit from buying goods abroad that are more costly to produce at home. **Competitive advantage** is the principle that makes international commerce work effectively. If a country does not have a competitive advantage in a product, there must be other reasons for that country to trade.

Command Economy

A command economy is one in which the government controls basic economic activities. Such an economy is directed by decisions of one group (the ruling class) for all members of the society. Such a system, typical in dictatorships, suffers because of the lack of private interest in economic success. Command economies are slower to respond to changing economic fluctuations, as they are controlled by cumbersome organizations and not responsive to the "invisible hand" of self-interest. Socialism and communism are examples of command economies today.

Marginalism

Marginalism concerns itself with the economic worth of the last (or next) product or service provided. The cost of making the last product, the cost of hiring the last employee, and the cost of selling the last product, determine the **marginal cost** of that next good. Presumably, a company will continue to produce goods and services until it becomes unprofitable. Production will cease when the marginal return of a product does not yield a profit. From the consumer's viewpoint, the **marginal utility** of the purchase is the crucial factor. How much satisfaction does an individual get from each purchase? When this marginal utility decreases too much, the buyer will not buy the next unit. The idea of diminishing returns often determines how many units of a good or service a buyer will purchase. For example, after eating a piece of pie, the want-satisfying power of the next piece of pie is decreased. When this marginal utility reaches a certain point, the consumer will stop buying.

Opportunity Cost

The opportunity cost of an economic decision is the loss of potential gain from other opportunities when one opportunity is taken. For example, a person may have enough money for a vacation in Europe or a new car but not both. The **opportunity cost** of buying the car will be the trip to Europe. These decisions are made usually on the **utility** of each choice. In other words, determining which choice would provide the most pleasure to the consumer. In a complex economy, there are many competing factors that provide utility. An individual, firm, or government will always choose what they perceive to be the best choice given limited resources. These choices are usually not clear-cut, and many factors go into some economic decisions. This is more common when companies or governments have to choose between a number of needed and attractive choices. Different parts of society will have different ideas about the best way to use their resources.

Criticisms of Marginality

Marginal utility is founded on **subjectivity**, rather than **objectivity**. Marginal utility places its focus on buying and selling transactions between individual units in the economy, to the exclusion of the activity of the economy as a whole. The marketplace is the Holy Grail for the proponents of marginal utility, who see the markets as the foundation of economic activity. The production function is ignored; this is a crucial error, as costs of production are a major determinant of prices, and, therefore, all microeconomic activity. Critics of marginal utility say it is impossible to understand **consumer utility**, which is determined in part by prices. The prices themselves are based on consumer preferences, making an accurate analysis difficult if not impossible. Another area of criticism for the concept of marginal utility is that it often attempts to correlate utility with price. This correlation does not hold true where a product may be useful and necessary to an individual but cost nothing. An example of this would be water.

Production in Depth

The production function in microeconomics refers to the total process of **producing or assembling** goods and services that are to be traded in a marketplace. Production decisions are some of the most vital in microeconomics. A firm or individual must decide what to make and how many units to provide. This will often depend on the method of production and the unit price of making each product. An evaluation of the necessary resources to be utilized is another important production decision. In tandem with sophisticated market research, optimum decisions can be made about producing goods and services. Production is a process, and, as such, it occurs through time and space. Because it is a flow concept, an important statistic is the amount of production for a specific period of time. Other factors of concern are the amount and physical dimensions of the finished process. This will be important in storing and shipping the finished goods.

Efficiency and X-Efficiency

The measurement of the productivity of a production process is vital. Productivity may be said to be **efficient** when the optimum number of finished products is produced with a minimum of raw materials, assuming quality control is maintained. If a production operation is less productive than anticipated, due to internal or external forces, it is said to be **X-efficient**. Such X-efficient production operations are often due to a number of factors beyond the control of the producer. Examples would be shortages of raw materials, increased and unexpected competition, or problems in the supply of necessary labor. The productivity of a production function is simply based on how many units of a finished product can be made from a minimum amount of inputs. The more efficient processes give firms an important competitive position and greater flexibility in pricing and marketing. Decisions made about production will often determine the success or failure of the product line for a firm.

Factors of Production

Factors of production are the sum total of the resources needed to produce finished goods. The major **factors** identified by economists include the use of land (for factories and agricultural products), labor (the human workforce), natural resources (raw materials used in manufacturing), and capital goods (previously manufactured equipment used in production). Human inputs such as management and human relations could be added to the mix. Contemporary economists often include technological expertise in the factors of production. Factors of production may be **fixed** (one which cannot be changed) or **variable** (one which can be adjusted by management easily). Examples of fixed factors would be physical plants, heavy machinery, and key managerial personnel. A variable factor of production is one whose usage rate can be changed easily. In the "long run" all of these factors of production can be adjusted by management. The "short run," however, is defined as a period in which at least one of the factors of production is fixed.

Diminishing Marginal Returns Analysis

As additional raw materials and resources are added to production factors, a point occurs where the production function becomes less efficient. In other words, additional resources are yielding less-profitable final products. This point is called the **point of diminishing returns** and is measured as a position on the marginal physical production curve. Continuing production will eventually result in producing products that lose money. Thus, it would be preferable to stop production. **Diminishing marginal returns** will vary from industry to industry, depending on the necessary factors of production needed to produce goods and services. The combination of land, labor, and capital needed for production is different for each product, so the point of diminishing marginal return will also differ. Demand, supply, and price changes in the factors of production will all impact this analysis.

Production Functions

Production functions, an important area of analysis in microeconomics, concerns itself with the ratio of raw materials or resources needed to produce a certain amount of goods and services. This relationship may be depicted as a mathematical one or illustrated with a graph. The goal of analyzing the production functions is to **optimize** the number of finished goods that can be obtained from the minimum of inputs. Many factors enter into such an analysis, including supply and demand of the factors of production, state-of-the-art technology, and managerial skill. Every production function will be different because of the mix of factors for producing different goods at various times. If a producer knows the exact quantity of finished goods he or she must manufacture, the **production function** would be the **minimum necessary resources** needed to achieve that production number. Current technology will affect this combination of resources. In this type of analysis, costs and prices are not considered.

Criticism

Controversy has surrounded the validity of production function analysis. Most of the **criticism** is concerned with how certain factors of production were measured and how proportions of the factors were mixed. Some economists feel it is not possible to post a necessary amount of capital without a complete understanding of both interest rates and the cost of labor. The production function analysis must include specific prices for all factors of production, but the analysis itself depends on knowing these variables. This is the "which came first, the chicken or the egg" problem. Exact variables cannot be known until the production function analysis is complete, but the analysis is the method of determining the variables. Special mathematical constructs and assumptions must be built in these models of production functioned to have a useful function.

Production Possibility Curve

When any product is made, there is an opportunity cost of forgoing using the resources to make a different product. If two or more items are being produced at the same time, there will be **opportunity costs** involved in decisions regarding the relative amount of each product to produce. This analysis is called the **production possibility curve**. The production possibility curve is a valuable tool for manufacturers because it explores production alternatives and their economic result. Points of **maximum productivity** may be plotted using this graphical tool, which will also illuminate when production becomes **inefficient**. Companies can then choose optimum mixes of products as well as determine when a finished good is not economically feasible to manufacture. The analysis should yield the necessary information for a firm to adjust their product mix and quantities of goods produced to the most profitable level.

Cost-Benefit Analysis

The determination of the best possible economic action in a situation is often formally or intuitively a result of a **cost-benefit computation**. An individual must ask what the total costs will be in any decision in relation to the total benefits, which may be reasonably predicted. Analyzing several alternatives using this approach will yield the best decision given the information available. In business decisions, this usually means determining what amount of resources must be used to gain a specified return or profit. Such cost-benefit calculations are not limited to money. Subjective factors must be considered and sometimes an arbitrary monetary value placed on them. Economic decisions, particularly on the part of governments, must weigh economic, quality-of-life, political, and social elements into this analysis. For example, a government decision to drill for oil in a natural habitat will include economic considerations, as well as the impact of the decision on the well-being of the society as a whole. Since almost all economic actions occur over time, future costs and profits must be considered from a **present-value perspective**.

Consumer Preference

Microeconomics is concerned with individual decisions that ultimately affect the entire economy. Consumer behavior is an important aspect of microeconomics. **Consumer preferences** are difficult to assess, because of the seemingly endless choices, conscious and unconscious, that motivate consumer behavior. Economic models have been constructed to better understand consumer activities. These are sometimes called **preference relations** (charting consumers' preferences). These models of consumer preferences have many flaws, but they can attempt to predict the behavior of buyers under various sets of conditions. A major flaw may be termed the completeness of understanding consumer behavior. Although a preference model may be able to show in theory how consumers will behave under a set of economic conditions, it is impossible to measure all the factors that enter into choices made by buyers. These choices are subject to rapid change due to external economic changes.

Determining Ideal Firm Size

Determining the optimum size of a company provides a challenge for managers. Because businesses are measured, in large part, by their profitability, the size of a firm should ideally be that which provides the **greatest profit**. This size will vary greatly between various companies, industries, and geographical locations. The ideal size of a firm is a fluid variable, changing with economic and competitive fluctuations. Economies and diseconomies of scale, scope, and agglomeration will all contribute to the determination of an **ideal business size**. Particular industries tend to affect the size of firms. For example, manufacturers of heavy equipment, with large labor and capital demands, tend to be larger than candy manufacturers, whose needs differ dramatically. Managers must constantly be attentive to their business' competitive position, costs, market share, and growth potential to adequately predict the ideal size of their companies. A fluid business environment makes these decisions difficult but crucial.

History of Money

Money has been defined as any store of value which has **intrinsic value** or is a **representation** of a store of value (banknotes). Money is the lifeblood of **market transactions**, serving as a measure of value, a medium of exchange, and a convention of accounting. As a means to exchange value for goods and services, money has no peer. But for this to be the case, money must have a guaranteed and obvious value of its own. Historically, commodities including crops and livestock were the first forms of money. When money became accepted as a representation of commodities, the market system was revolutionized. It made trading easy, and quickly became an accepted medium of exchange. In earlier times, money represented the commodities of precious metals, notably gold and silver. In modern economies, money depends on the guarantee of the government to honor its value. These guarantees permit international trade without risk about the value of the money involved.

Forms of Money

The first items considered as "money" were commodities that were traded under a **barter system**. The next advance in the form of money was the minting of **coins** of precious metals, usually silver and gold. This form of money had intrinsic value but was a very limited resource. It could be transported fairly easily in moderate amounts and was difficult to forge. The next leap in the form of money was the advent of **paper notes**, issued and guaranteed by governments. In modern economies, money has taken on a variety of new forms, some a result of increasing technological advances. Modern economies feature paper notes backed by the central bank and government that issues them. Coins with a small percentage of silver or gold are also assets honored by central banks. The intrinsic value of precious metals in most coins is negligible. By far the most revolutionary change in the form of money has occurred in the last 100 years. Demand deposits, credit cards, commercial paper, certificates of deposit, mortgages, and public and private promissory notes are all a form of money today.

John Maynard Keynes

Perhaps the most influential economist of the last 100 years was **John Maynard Keynes**. Born in 1883, Keynes lived his life and developed his theories in England during the first quarter of the 20th century. Although a great proponent of government intervention in managing the economy, Keynes was strongly opposed to socialism, which he felt would weaken a free economy. Keynes's major concerns were the management and control of business cycles, eliminating both depressions and inflation, which he saw as destabilizing economic systems. His major thesis was that **aggregate demand** was the most important indicator of economic cycles, particularly the extremes of depression and runaway inflation.

Keynes summarized his theories in *The General Theory of Employment, Interest, and Money*, which he wrote in the early 1930s. Keynes's ideas gained international acclaim and were the basis for the active government role in combating the depression in the 1930s. His ideas appeal to those who believe the responsibility of the government is to act strongly to encourage economic growth.

Robert Lucas Jr.

Robert Lucas Jr. is regarded as one of the most important contemporary economists. A professor of Economics at the University of Chicago, Lucas was instrumental in applying microeconomic analytical methods to study the economy as a whole. His work on the theory of "**Rational Expectations**" was groundbreaking and added greatly to his reputation as a leading economist. He was awarded the Nobel Prize for this work in 1995. The "**Lucas Technique**" investigates the dynamic relationships in an economy. It analyzes the cause-and-effect determination of such economic indicators as employment, inflation, government policies in economics, and the role of monetary policy in affecting economic activity. Creator of the famous "**Lucas islands**" model of monetary influence among consumers, he has earned a place of international respect from economists all over the world. Lucas remains an active researcher and economic theorist today.

Robert Mundell

Robert Mundell is another leading contemporary macroeconomist. A professor at Columbia University, Mundell is a leading figure in the development of **supply-side economics**. He was awarded the Nobel Prize in Economics in 1999 for his overall contributions to economic theory. Mundell pioneered theory on **optimal currency areas**, which reflected his interest in the role of currencies in the economic fluctuations of countries. This work established him as an expert on money and currency, and Mundell was active in the development of the **euro** for the European Union. His work in advocating supply-side economics is well known, and he is known as a leading expert on the gold standard and its historical implications. Mundell was hailed as a prophet when he accurately predicted the rampant inflation of the 1970s. He has developed several important economic models, including the **Mundell-Fleming model** and the **Mundell-Tobin effect**.

Finn Erling Kydland

A Norwegian economist who won the Nobel Prize in Economics in 2004 for his research and models of macroeconomic systems, **Kydland** currently holds a teaching position at the University of California. Kydland has immersed himself in the study of the impact of government economic policy over a period of years. His work on the understanding of the **fluctuations of business cycles** is classic, and he is regarded as a pioneer in applying **mathematical models** to the analysis of economic activity. A leading thinker in political economy and macroeconomics, Kydland has done primary and secondary research on the effects of fiscal and monetary policy on business cycles. Labor economics is another specialty of his, and he is regarded as one of the most important of the labor economists. The relationships between the availability, cost, and demand for labor on economic cycles are of paramount interest to Kydland.

Edward Prescott

A major macroeconomist of the day is **Edward Prescott**. A close collaborator of Finn Kydland, with whom he shared the Nobel Prize in economics in 2004, Prescott currently serves as an economist for the Federal Reserve System. He has concentrated his economic interests in the areas of **general equilibrium** and **fluctuations of economic activity**. His particular field of interest is the role of central banks in applying monetary policy to affect business cycles. He addresses the question of whether central banks should be given wide-ranging power to increase or decrease the money supply in an attempt to avoid economic extremes. Prescott developed the **Hodrick-Prescott model of strategies** to even the ups and downs of business cycles. This was widely hailed by economists as a major breakthrough in the management of economic fluctuations in an economy. Prescott currently engages in monetary and fiscal research, as well as holding several teaching positions in economics.

Developmental Economics

Developing countries have unique economic problems that more sophisticated economies do not. Particularly important is the area of long-term economic growth in developing economies. This field is called **developmental economics**. It also includes the microeconomic analyses of individuals and firms in such fledgling economies. It is a highly analytical field that uses **econometrics** (mathematical applications to economics) to predict economic patterns. Usually, both mathematical and qualitative tools are used to measure and predict economic activity in developing countries. Included in the field are the problems of long-term debt and the action of international economic agencies such as the International Monetary Fund. The problem of encouraging and sustaining economic growth in such countries is a primary objective of economists. The field includes not only economic issues and tools but also social and political methods to influence the whole society.

Political Economy

Political economics is an umbrella term that includes a wide variety of economic approaches to study and predict behavior. It often uses techniques and tools from other social sciences in its applications. **Political economy** is a maverick in economic theory, as it often contravenes accepted economic doctrine. Interdisciplinary by definition, political economy studies the interactions of social and political factors on economic issues that affect markets. The term was originally used in political science to compare and contrast relationships of geopolitics between countries. A number of political-social-economic schools have made political economy their main interest. The historical long-term implications of political economy are of great interest to economic historians.

Transport, Exchange, Infrastructure, and Consumption

Transportation is the network that allows the economy to function. Capital and labor must be moved to land in order to facilitate production. Finished goods must be moved through channels of distribution to be available to consumers. **Transport** is necessary for the movement of products, people, and capital. **Economic exchange** is the basic activity of economics. The circular cycle of exchange from consumer to suppliers and back are the transactions that move an economy. The field of exchange is the marketplace, and money is the medium through which these transactions move. Building an **infrastructure** for market transactions is necessary to allow an orderly and dependable mechanism for economic exchange. **Consumption** of goods, services, and ancillary products is the final activity for satisfying the needs and wants of society. Consumption also may include the less tangible qualities of health, leisure activity, goodwill, and freedom of choice.

Disposal

All excess products of consumption or production must be eliminated as **waste**. The failure to dispose of these waste products will result in an impaired economy and a degradation of the quality of life. Waste removal requires a large physical capacity and the employment of significant capital resources. The increasing urbanization of the world makes **waste disposal** an important priority. Systems of waste removal include garbage and sewage operations as well as preventative measures of recycling and legislation to protect the environment. Governments must take responsibility for waste removal because of the scope of the problem. The ecological movement and "green" economics of the past 30 years have raised questions on the economics of waste and the quality of life. This has generated increased concern about such issues as destruction of natural habitats, global warming, air and water pollution, and the importance of sustaining our natural resources.

"The Market"

The central arena of political economy is the **marketplace** where economic activity occurs. It is also the intersecting point of the sometimes competing economic interests and forces at play. Common causes may be found by unlikely allies, and groups may be pitted against each other for economic advantage. In a **capitalistic economic system**, the major task of the state is the creation and preservation of capital and the economic choices involved in its allocation. **Socialism** maintains that decisions and implementation of production should be determined by the power of the state, ostensibly to create the greatest good for the most people. This philosophy brings socialism into conflict with capitalism, which requires that fundamental economic power should be in private hands. **Communism** seeks control over all factors of production as well as political and social dominance over its society.

"Adaptive Expectations"

When individuals base their expectations on past economic events and history, it is called "**adaptive expectations.**" An example would be if the stock market has been strong for a period of time, the public will have positive expectations for future advances. Individuals will base their future economic decisions on the cumulative experience of recent economic activity. These decisions will become self-fulfilling if consumers are pessimistic about the future of the economy. An example of adaptive expectations is the general attitude regarding inflation. In the United States, as well as most of the free world, inflation has become a fact of economic life. The expectation of rising prices, increasing wages, and general cost-of-living increases has bred a culture of inflationary expectation that rarely fails to materialize. Sometimes, general pessimism about the economy serves as a deterrent to economic expansion. This is another example of adaptive expectations at work.

Gresham's Law

When two or more types of money are commonly used in an economy, and each is assigned the same value by the country, problems may arise. **Thomas Gresham**, a 15th-century English financial genius, stated that money that has a market value lower than its buying power will drive out a form of money that has **stronger consumption value**. People will tend to keep this "good money" as a store of value and spend the "bad money" to exchange for goods and services. This situation can only happen if two different forms of money are in circulation and the state decrees them to have equal value, when in fact they do not. Given a choice of exchanging good or bad money for goods and services people will always spend the bad money and retain the good money. Thus, as **Gresham's law** states, bad money will drive good money out of circulation. This becomes a serious economic problem if people are hoarding good money as a store of value and using bad money in the marketplace. Soon, all the good money will disappear as people hoard it.

Consumption

When a resource is used and eliminated, it has been **consumed**. Consumption is an important feature of economics, usually meaning personal consumption of goods and services. Consumption has its own determinants, including economic expectations, level of disposable income, and the propensity to consume. Ultimately consumption is a component of aggregate demand in economic theory. Economics makes a clear distinction between **production**, the supplying of goods and services, and the **consumption** of these goods and services. Economic research into consumption raises questions regarding the motivation and reasons for various levels of consumption. The relatively recent importance of our consumer society has placed this element of economic theory under the microscope of analysis. Consumption in all its forms has developed a significant impact on the lives of everyone in a modern economy.

Labor Economics

As in all the factors of production, **labor** has a separate market based on supply and demand. The interaction between employers and workers is the frame of reference of **labor economics**. The result of these interactions affect labor economics and determine income, employment, and wage levels. Labor economics is a vital field since most countries include maximized employment as an economic priority. When labor economics is studied through the individuals and their role in labor markets, microeconomic methods are used. The larger interactions between labor markets and the demand for goods and services, production, consumption, and investment fall under macroeconomic analysis. Both are necessary and useful methods for evaluating the role that labor plays in economic activity. Most of us are more aware of the macroeconomics of labor, which tends to be in the news more often as trends of unemployment and productivity.

Commodity Markets

Commodities are raw or unfinished components of finished goods yet to be produced. Agricultural products such as soybeans, cotton, and wheat are commodities. Separate markets exist for almost all commodities. Currencies of various countries are also traded as commodities in their own markets. Futures markets exist on many heavily traded commodities, where speculation fuels trading for future delivery of products paid for now. Commodities were one of the first classes of goods traded between countries. Modern **commodity markets** have been safeguarded by a bevy of rules and regulations ensuring prompt and accurate payment between countries. International agencies, such as the Bank for International Settlements, regulate transaction settlements, insure currencies, set reserve requirements, and generally reduce risks in trade inherent between countries.

Store of Value

Any form of money or capital including commodities may be seen as a **store of value** if it meets certain standards. Any store of value must be readily stored, retrieved, and saved. The store of value must retain its value over time, both as intrinsic wealth and the ability to use it to settle debts. Many assets have been used as a store of value over the centuries. Precious metals, primarily gold and silver, have been historical favorites. The most stable currencies extant at a historical point also may serve as a store of value. When the British Empire was powerful, the pound sterling was often used as the store of value. Real estate has always been known as a reliable store of value, and art, antiques, and rare collections have also served this purpose. Many of these are not practical for daily trading, which includes immediate settling of accounts. The common feature is that they all have **intrinsic value** and rarely lose it. There is always a more or less stable demand for these items.

High Technology Economics

Many economists and investors feel that the sector of the economy using cutting-edge **high technological methods** is the most promising for economic growth. This conclusion has promoted increasing and sometimes speculative investment in high-tech fields. But as the world learned from the anticipated boom in information technology, reality does not always meet expectations. The so-called "dot-com" boom in the last 20 years saw the making of great fortunes but also the loss of investments when companies failed to meet their expected growth. High technology economics still offers uncommon rewards for the astute investor, but must also be regarded as very high risk for investors. Areas usually associated with high technology advances include nanotechnology, information technology, and biotechnology, among many others. High technology industries flourish across the world, making constant progress in developing new techniques and applications for multiple growth industries.

The Invisible Hand

One of the fundamental concepts of classical economics is the "**invisible guiding hand of self-interest**" that posits each individual will make economic decisions based on his or her best interests. Developed by **Adam Smith**, the father of capitalism and leading classical economist, the theory states that individuals acting in their own self-interest will also promote the general welfare of all members of the society. Smith felt this was a social mechanism that tended to benefit all. Smith's argument was based on his belief that in a free market economy, people tend to produce goods in demand by consumers. He did not necessarily feel that all self-interested action by itself benefited all of society. Smith's original observations and conclusions are a foundation of classical economics and have been incorporated in one form or another in many schools of economics. Much of **macroeconomic theory** uses the invisible hand concept in postulating economic behavior.

Cost-Of-Production Theory of Value

The concept that the value of an object represents the sum total of all the resources that were involved in producing it is called the **cost-of-production theory of value**. This cost would include any and all of the factors of production utilized in producing the good. Classical economists support the **labor theory-of-value** ideas of Adam Smith, David Ricardo, and Karl Marx. Marx's theory is flawed by his inclusion of the surplus component of value unrelated to the production process. Most contemporary economists reject the cost-of-production theory of value in favor of the marginal theory of value, which contends that an economic value is determined by the marginal utility derived by the consumer in using the product. Some economists distinguish between sectors with **cost-determined** prices and values and **demand-determined** value, which is set by the level of aggregate demand.

Laissez-Faire

The term *laissez-faire* is derived from the French imperative *lassier faire*, meaning to "let do," indicating a hands-off approach. Historically, the term was used by the physiocrats who demanded less governmental influence on international trade. It has become a catch-all phrase for allowing the market the freedom inherent in transactions, without outside influences. Classical economics found a supporter for ***laissez-faire*** in Adam Smith, although he had reservations about some aspects of the policy. A broader definition of *laissez-faire* reflects a style of leadership that allows maximum freedom of individuals to act on their own initiative rather than following orders routinely. It empowers subordinates to make independent decisions and take action on their own. Critics of *laissez-faire* economics point out the failures of lack of any control on economic affairs. The 1920s are sometimes cited as a period in which a lack of government safeguards plunged the country into the Great Depression.

INFORMATION ECONOMICS

The sub-branch of economics which deals with the use of information in making economic policy and decisions is called **information economics**. Information has unique qualities, being wildly inaccurate at times, easily accessible, and difficult to fully believe. A prime element in economic decisions, information makes accurate and valid choices difficult at times. Information economics studies the mechanisms of economic technology, the value of economic information and its applications, and the asymmetries of information in economics. The market for information is unique. Information is presumably for sale to anyone who will buy it, and it can be sold multiple times. Information has virtually no marginal cost to the buyer. It is easy to duplicate and may be resold many times over. Sometimes information is sold as a bundle. Various sources and pieces of information are combined and sold with or without commentary or suggestions.

REAGANOMICS

The term *Reaganomics* is an umbrella description of the economic policy of the Reagan administration from 1980-1988. These policies faced very high inflation rates and increasing unemployment, a combination called **stagflation**. These dual problems were addressed by applying the principles of **supply-side economics**, combining tax reductions with decreased government spending. Liberal economists and politicians bemoaned the approach as helping the wealthy at the expense of middle- and lower-income individuals. Supply-side economics attempts to encourage investment and expansion through tax cuts and austerity programs rather than stimulating demand. This is the idea of the "trickle-down" approach of economic well-being, beginning at the top. The twin problems of inflation and unemployment were largely solved during the Reagan years, but there is hot debate whether this was caused by economic policy or simply a turn in the business cycle.

THOMAS MALTHUS AND "DISMAL SCIENCE"

Thomas Malthus, the 18th-century economist who named economics the "**dismal science**," felt that population would grow at a rate that would cause people to starve, and the level of population would reach a subsistence level. Malthus's theories have been proved wrong in a large part of the developed world, but his predictions are accurate for many poor third-world countries who suffer periodic **famines**. Industrialized countries have developed technologies to produce food to keep abreast of population growth, which has been slowed by birth control methods. Developing countries with unchecked population explosions and inferior technology often cannot produce enough food to feed themselves. These countries must rely on international aid and relief agencies to provide the essentials of life. Much of the development of third-world nations is geared to increasing food production and introducing methods to slow the population growth. These actions have had mixed success to date.

SIGNIFICANT LITERATURE IN ECONOMICS

THE WEALTH OF NATIONS - ADAM SMITH

The book is usually considered to be the beginning of **modern economics**. It begins with a discussion of the Industrial Revolution. Later, it critiques mercantilism and a synthesis of the emerging economic thinking of his time. It is mostly known due to the idea of **The Invisible Hand**, which means that people will unintentionally improve their community through the pursuit of their own wants and needs.

Das Kapital - Karl Marx

Das Kapital is a political-economic treatise by Karl Marx. The book is a critical analysis of **capitalism** and of the political economy practices during his time. Marx bases his work on that of the classical economists like Adam Smith, David Ricardo, and even Benjamin Franklin.

General Theory of Employment, Interest and Money -John Maynard Keynes

The General Theory of Employment, Interest and Money is generally considered to be the masterwork of the English economist John Maynard Keynes. To a great extent, it created the terminology of **modern macroeconomics**. The book ushered in a new age of economic thinking, referred to as the "**Keynesian Revolution**."

Bank Regulations

Since the failure of hundreds of banks during the great depression, the **solvency** of commercial banks has become a responsibility of government. **Demand deposits** are insured by agencies of the government so a depositor is protected from losing assets if a bank should fail. Of course, the major objective of banking regulations is to prevent failures. To maintain the integrity of the banking system, federal and state governments have required commercial banks to follow certain rules and regulations. The most important of these requirements is to ensure banks reserve a certain percentage of their demand deposits as a reserve asset, ensuring that banks do not overextend themselves with loans. Today, only transaction deposits are subject to this rule. This regulation protects depositors against bank insolvency, as does the federal government's insurance plans. The Federal Reserve imposes capital guidelines for commercial banks and savings banks, which provide regulations on certain types of loans. These guidelines are risk-based and protect banks from making poor decisions on a borrower's ability to repay the loan.

Savings

Technically, in economic theory, disposable income is either **consumed** or **saved**. The amount left over when goods and services have been purchased by consumers is considered to be savings. Other categories of savings include corporations' retained earnings and a government surplus. The definition of the term *savings* is subject to various interpretations. Individuals who repay loans of any kind rather than consuming the income are really saving. Interest paid on loans is not savings, but must be counted as income by those who receive the interest. A differentiation must be made between saving, which is to increase assets, and savings, which is one element of a person's total net worth. To save is an activity that results in additional net worth as a separate category. Although this may seem to be a differentiation without a difference, the terms have separate meanings in economic analysis and should be understood in economic terms.

Investments

Investment and savings are two sides of the same coin. If a decision is made to save, the opportunity cost of consumption is sacrificed. Savings can be utilized to **reinvest** in land, capital improvements, and equipment. This type of saving increases the total capita and promotes economic expansion. Savings does not automatically equal **investment**, because both of these decisions are made by different entities in an economy and often for different purposes. It is possible to save yet not increase investment, which can result in a decline in demand, which further leads to increased unemployment, reduction in production, and a business cycle that can lead to recession or depression. This has been named the **paradox of thrift**, because saving more would seem to be a positive spur to the economy, while in many cases it is not. However, when investment increases over savings, aggregate demand is stimulated, and the business cycle may turn toward expansion.

Other Meanings of Investment in Aspects of Finance and Economics

Although investment has a technical meaning in economic theory, it has several other definitions that apply to aspects of finance and economics. In everyday language, we speak of investment as a **speculation** for future gain. Common types of investments are stocks, bonds, government securities, mutual funds, insurance policies, commodities, and real estate. Markets exist in many forms for various types of investments. **Formal exchanges** are the rule in security investing, examples including the New York Stock Exchange and the American Stock Exchange. Investments such as stocks and bonds may provide income in interest and dividends and offer the promise of **appreciation**. Less tangible markets exist for countless items, such as coins, stamps, and markets for professional athletes. Trading in **securities** has become much easier through internet buying and selling. Investment clubs are common in society, and colleges and universities allow students to manage funds as part of their training.

Interest Rates

There are several ways to view interest rates in economics. Interest is the cost of using money in formal analysis. It is the cost of using **capital**. Keynes felt that **interest rates** did not affect saving or investment, as had been believed by classical economists. Classical economics taught that interest rates would adjust toward equilibrium and directly influence savings and investment decisions. As in most areas of economics, the **demand** for and the **supply** of money determine interest rates. The rate of interest will fluctuate depending on many economic variables. Finance employs the term *interest rates* to designate a charge for borrowing money. Interest may also be considered a return on an investment, the interest rate determining the return. It is actually a rate of return on a capital investment. An investor rents money and is charged a percentage of the value of the investment as the cost of borrowing.

Transfer Payments

A transfer payment in economic jargon is any transfer of money from one element of an economy to another, in which there is no expected reciprocal return. Examples of **transfer payments** abound in an economy. Social security transfers, disability and unemployment benefits, and any payment from a government agency for which the recipient does nothing are all forms of transfer payments. Scholarships and interest-free loans are also transfer payments. Transfer payments can also flow between levels of government. Federal disaster relief, subsidies of all kinds, and direct transfers of monies for a multitude of purposes fall into the category of transfer payments. Even state and local taxes are transfer payments in the sense that they are paid by businesses and individuals without getting anything in direct return. Of course, many of the state and municipal functions are providing an indirect return to taxpayers in the form of essential services rendered.

Standard of Deferred Payments

In any transaction, there must be a currency or commodity that is generally accepted as a means of settling debt. **Deferred payment** for a current transaction to be settled later are guided by the standard used at the time. Historically, gold and silver were used as the standard of deferred payments, because they had intrinsic value and everyone could agree on their worth. When the gold standard was in effect, all currencies were guaranteed to be exchanged at a **fixed rate**. In modern economics, the strongest currencies usually serve as the standard of deferred payment. Today, the United States dollar and the European Union's euro are considered the most reliable standard of deferred payment. Illegal transactions rarely allow deferred payments, but if they do, compensation may be made in gold or diamonds, whose store of value is unquestioned. The instability of money at a given time makes the deferred standard of payment more important.

International Monetary Fund

The **international financial network** is a huge and complex array of associations and organizations representing governments, businesses, and individuals. This includes a bewildering number of markets featuring ever-changing exchange rates and fluctuating conditions in the world's economy. Overseeing and monitoring this system is the **International Monetary Fund**. The IMF stands by as a consultant and watchdog over exchange markets and the resulting balance of payments account of participating countries. The IMF is governed by 190 member countries, joining in a cooperative effort to control international markets and avoid financial instability. The institution has grown dramatically since its inception when only 44 countries were included in the charter. Presently, the IMF provides an important role in helping developing nations gain stable economies. Increased membership and the problems of new countries such as those created with the breakup of the Soviet Union have made the role of the IMF an increasingly important one in the world.

Criticisms

As may have been anticipated, the **International Monetary Fund** has become an object of criticism since its charter. One accusation is that the IMF has been partial toward countries that have friendly relations with the United States and other Western powers. Liberal and radical critics accuse the IMF of supporting countries with dictatorships and ignoring complaints regarding civil liberties and human rights in these nations. Defenders of the IMF respond that the organization is an economic group, not a political one. They contend that before a democracy or republic can flourish, it must have a stable economy. The debate continues with liberal politicians supporting the proactive policies of the IMF in stabilizing economies, while more conservative observers feel that supply-side policy would allow the economies of developing nations to grow unimpeded by government intervention. The tendency of the IMF to promote currency devaluation is particularly aggravating to conservative economists and politicians alike.

The World Bank

History

The World Bank was chartered in 1944, when the post-World War II devastation of economies was a major global concern. The organization addressed the problems of rebuilding the economies of Western Europe and providing stability for international investment in those countries (as well as other developing nations). In recent decades, the **World Bank** has become an active participant in reducing poverty and promoting economic growth in **third-world countries**. Included in the economic support is the improvement of education, farming, and manufacturing technology. The major financial tool of the World Bank is to provide funds through **loans** to these countries. The loans usually carry a much lower interest rate than what normally would be charged. The World Bank is actually an association of five separate but related agencies working toward a common goal. It is highly regarded as an organization of integrity by economists and governments alike.

Goals

The work of the World Bank is to provide financial and consulting support for **developing countries**. The problems of dire poverty and famine are common in these countries, and the World Bank is active in attempting to solve these problems. It's tools are primarily financial, but the World Bank serves as an economic resource for financial planning for these countries. Funds are loaned at preferable interest rates to build or repair infrastructure of countries, as well as promote social and economic reforms. Environmental issues are important to the World Bank in making loans and supporting third-world countries. A new emphasis on reducing poverty has influenced recent policy at the World Bank. This includes the advocacy for individual businesses to rebuild flagging economies. Broader goals have been related to the improvement of the standard of living through the promotion of reduced pollution, education, and the creation of entities capable of sustainable growth over time.

Criticisms

Although the World Bank has a generally good reputation in global economics, it is not without its critics. The crux of these concerns is that many of their programs include provisions that alter the structure of the society and rob it of its **autonomy**. Almost always, the World Bank promotes economic liberation from archaic practices, which are sometimes deeply ingrained in the society of a country. These policies often reduce the power of a nation in managing its own economy, in the interest of promoting the general welfare.

Another related criticism of the World Bank is its liberal and progressive political stance. The Bank often requires countries to accept certain conditions as a requisite for financial aid. Sometimes, critics argue that these requirements include reforms not appropriate for unstable governments and countries in conflict. The influence of the United States is often thought to be excessive, and this causes policy that would favor American economic and political interests. Examples include the introduction of foreign businesses to compete with local industries.

Problems with Equating GDP Per Capita and Economic Well-Being

Several economic factors may interfere with equating GDP per capita with individual well-being. A significant allocation of assets is used to combat the negative effects of economic growth such as the destruction of natural habitats and air and water pollution. Economic growth increases such **intangibles** as the increase in commuting, which affects quality of life. Perhaps most importantly, GDP does not account for a significant amount of **domestic production,** such as child-raising and homemaking. The money equivalents for these tasks are omitted from the GDP calculation. There are numerous markets that are left out of GDP, including black markets, criminal activity, and alternative economies. There is also no provision in GDP for volunteer activity, "do it yourself" tasks such as home improvements and landscape management. All of these economic activities are omitted from the formal measurement of per capita GDP and fail to give an accurate picture of individual well-being.

Unemployment in Capitalism

Unemployment in a free market situation occurs only in **capitalistic** economic systems. In Fascism, Socialism, and Communism, the factors of production, including labor, are under the direct control of the **state**. Historically, precapitalist societies such as feudalism formed the basis for the economy. In this case, the serfs were all employed (if able) by mandate of the lords. More primitive societies such as tribes view the entire group as part of one family and take responsibility for ensuring all are cared for adequately. Debate continues on the necessary and appropriate action of governments in curbing unemployment. Liberal and welfare economists often call for a more active role for government in increasing employment, while more conservative analysts feel government intervention exacerbates the problem by its interference. Laws forbidding strikes and layoffs are cited as inappropriate government action to solve unemployment.

Economic Indicators

Business or economic indicators are specific measurements that are used to predict the future course of the economy. They are used as analytical tools to measure and forecast economic activity and future behavior of the economy. Common **economic indicators** are indexes, compilations of data, summaries of economic activity in a period of time, and statistics measuring the level of consumption, investment, savings, and unemployment in the economy. Fluctuations in the money supply and industrial output are important indicators. Measurements for inflation, retail sales, and stock market prices provide supporting data. The National Bureau of Economic Research, whose prime interest is in predicting business cycles, provides many of the important economic indicators used for forecasting. When an indicator occurs behind economic activity, it is called a **lagging indicator**. Indicators current with economic activity are known as **coincident indicators**.

Economic Policy Goals and Tools

Governments and economies usually set **goals** for their economic plans and policy decisions. Goals may be short-term or long-term, and they tend to focus on big-picture elements such as inflation control, employment levels, and economic growth rates. These policy goals are implemented with economic tools that include monetary and fiscal policy, increases or decreases in government spending, international trade practices, regulation of labor markets, and many additional methods. Often, goals are not exclusively economic, as with defense and other areas of the general welfare. A government must determine which short-term goals are most important to its policy. It may be impossible to reduce inflation while promoting more employment at the same time. Governments are usually more successful with a few short-term goals that work with each other to affect long-term goals. A consistent policy approach to economic problems is essential to achieve economic goals.

Microeconomics

Subsidies

In economics, a subsidy is a unilateral transfer of money, usually by a government institution, artificially supporting the price of a commodity based on the importance of that good to the general welfare. **Subsidies** take various forms, including direct cash payments, letters of credit, or tax incentives. Subsidies guarantee the producer a better price than may be obtained on the open market. They correspondingly reduce the consumer price but at a cost to the free operation of the market. Subsidies skew demand and supply curves and encourage consumers to spend rather than save. This hurts the economy and the consumers by causing overconsumption because of an artificially lower price. Subsidies have historically been used for agricultural products, particularly under governments attempting to increase income to producers. Subsidies were used heavily during the New Deal and Fair Deal to help selected groups in the economy.

Trade Between Nations

Commerce between nations, the trading of products and service functions from one country to another, is called **international trade**. Trade between countries was very limited in the premodern era. As the capabilities for shipping and transport increased, so did the opportunities for international commerce. Today, it constitutes a significant portion of many countries' economies. The rise of companies doing business in many countries has contributed to the increase of international trade. The term "**globalization**" has come to mean the spreading network of economic ties throughout the world. International trade is used as a political as well as economic strategy in relations between nations. As countries seek new markets in order to grow and prosper, international commerce is an ideal avenue for economic growth. **Tariff policy** is another weapon used in geopolitics as nations strive to prosper in an increasingly competitive world. Economic success for many individual firms depends on their ability to develop international markets for their goods and services.

Potential Economic Risks in International Trade

The primary risks in international trade are **economic** in nature. Care must be taken in international commerce to accurately assess the economic stability of the buyer. Trade partners must have confidence in the liquidity of their counterparts and be assured that the buyer has the continued means to meet his obligations. This confidence fosters an atmosphere where international commerce can grow and flourish. Countries must believe that they have not lost control of their economic destiny by trading freely. Another related area of concern is the **geopolitical arena**. Economic policy is a powerful tool that can be used as a political weapon. Concerns about trading with potential enemies as well as possible confiscation during periods of international strife are real. Firms may become dependent on certain licenses to engage in international business, and fear the revocation of these agreements. The uncertainty of foreign exchange rates and stability of trading partners' economies remain realistic concerns in today's global economy.

Balance of Trade

Every country hopes to have a positive **balance of trade.** This means they have sold more goods and services abroad than they have purchased. Such a positive balance of trade (called a **surplus**) indicates a strong economy with good international markets. Conversely, a **negative balance of trade** (called a **deficit**) can indicate some fundamental weakness in a country's ability to profitably engage in international commerce. Trade restrictions, including tariffs and other regulations, can weaken a country's trading position. Widely fluctuating exchange rates may cast uncertainty on the wisdom of trading with a particular country. Social and political environments have a direct effect on international commerce. Basic economic indicators such as inflation, price levels, and aggregate demand and supply all have a bearing on the balance of payments. Ultimately, it is the totality of all these issues that may determine the success of a country in international business.

Utility Function and Neoclassical Economics

Neoclassical economists consider the **utility function** paramount in most economic and non-economic choices of individuals and states. This includes both short-term and long-term economics. This theory of economic behavior extends to decisions made daily by consumers. What to consume and at what cost are the driving forces of microeconomics. Understanding that consumption choices involve opportunity costs is implicit in the economic choices made. **Neoclassical economists** tend to favor what has been termed supply-side economics, focusing on providing incentives to individuals and businesses rather than attempting to manipulate demand. **Monetarism** attempts to influence economic activity and growth through increasing or decreasing the money supply in an economy. Proponents of this philosophy tend to reject direct government intervention in the economy.

Modeling and Economic Reasoning

The development of a methodology and logistical framework for discussion and argument has been an important step in the development of economics as a science. Modern economics has utilized new information gathering and processing technologies that expedite and organize the compilation of economic information. Much more detailed data is now available as the raw material for economic methodology. The application of **modeling** to economics has provided a framework for the application of the scientific method to economics, to study economic behavior and test hypotheses. Modeling allows the creation of artificial relationships to measure and manipulate economic activities. Models mirror the real world of economics and provide an opportunity for economists to systematically study economic relationships. As more sophisticated methods of study have evolved, the application of mathematics to economics, termed *econometrics*, has yielded more accurate and useful information in economic methodology.

Microeconomic Theory

The development of economic theory as it relates to individual units in a society is called **microeconomics**. These units may be individuals, firms, labor forces, resource pools, and consumers. The behavior of both people and businesses is included in microeconomics. The term itself means "small-scale" economics. Microeconomics questions how the activities of small units in an economy interact, and theorizes about the implications of such transactions. The utilization of scarce resources by individuals and firms is a central topic in microeconomics. Models of the marketplace where households and commercial companies interact and trade are key components in microeconomics. Economic activity is sometimes viewed as a process between corporations, businesses, and individuals. This process illustrates the mechanisms of a market economy when studied from small individual units within that economy. Relationships between scarce assets, such as natural resources, money, labor, and the factors of production are all easily visualized from the individual level of economics.

Principles of Supply and Demand

A competitive market is composed of buyers and sellers engaged in trade in an organized manner. The price and the number of products sold are determined by the **supply** of and **demand** for the goods or services. **Microeconomics** is the study of these market factors to understand and predict market activity. A central tenet of the market is the rise in price when demand exceeds supply of a good or service. However, when supply exceeds demand for a good or service, the price will fall. The constant flux of demand, supply, and price always tends toward **equilibrium**, when supply and demand equal each other. In real economic systems, this point is rarely reached, and if so, only briefly. In a complex economy where there are endless choices to be made, demand and supply only occasionally reach an equilibrium. Elements of economic choice and the opportunity cost of such choices make it very difficult for demand and supply to be equal for a particular good or service.

Market Equilibrium

The condition of market equilibrium is achieved when demand for a good or service equals the amount of that product made available by suppliers. Any organized market tends to work toward a state of **equilibrium**, as the forces of supply and demand fluctuate over time. Shortages may occur, causing increased demand and higher prices. The higher prices will reduce demand, causing prices to drop as the market moves toward equilibrium. The equilibrium point is rarely, if ever, actually attained, since the endless changes in supply, demand, and fluctuating prices create some imbalance between supply and demand. Despite this reality, it is important to note that a free market is always working toward this equilibrium state. The economic behavior of buyers and sellers will move the market in the direction of balance between demand and supply.

Results of Shortage

When a good or service is demanded in excess of the ability of the supplier to meet this demand, a **shortage** will occur. A shortage will drive the **demand** for a product or service up, and **prices** will rise. Shortages can be artificially manufactured by suppliers to manipulate the market. An example of this occurred in the 1970s when OPEC chose to limit the production of oil in order to increase demand, and thus raise prices. This proved to be an effective strategy, as Americans who depended on gasoline increased demand and prices rose because of the shortage. When OPEC increased the production of oil after political pressure was applied, supplies of gasoline returned to normal and prices fell. The market again moved toward equilibrium as the artificial manipulation of the supply of oil ended. This episode drove home the point that to depend on a few suppliers of a necessary product leaves consumers open to manipulated shortages.

MARKETS AND PERFECTLY COMPETITIVE MARKETS

Markets may be located physically in particular places, such as a produce market, or may be intangible, such as a market for fine art. All markets operate under an implied agreement between buyers and sellers on trading for goods and services at specified but fluctuating prices. Markets provide the laboratory where economic theory and practice may be observed and studied. Anywhere that goods are offered for sale and buyers exist, a **market** is said to be present. A **specialized** type of market is one in which all products are the same and everyone has equal access to market information. Such a market is said to be **perfectly competitive** when it reaches a significant size. The size must be large enough that individual units of the market (buyers and sellers) are unable to determine the price of the goods or services by themselves. In such a market, perfect competition may be said to exist. Practically, perfectly competitive markets are uncommon, due to a myriad of factors that affect a given market.

PRICE AND PRICE THEORY

A free market depends on a system of value to measure the scope and action of an economic system. **Price** is the traditional measurement of value between sellers and buyers in a market. **Price theory** measures the relationship between prices and other economic variables in a market economy. Price theory has demonstrated the importance of prices on both demand and supply in economic analysis. The demand for resources is a derived demand, based on demand for the products that require the resources for their production. The greater the demand for the final products of the resources the higher the price of those resources. Thus, resources are priced just as goods and services are priced: according to the demand and supply for the resources. It follows that the price of final goods and services depends in large part on the price of the resources needed to supply the final product.

PRICE DISCRIMINATION

When a supplier of the same goods and services uses a multitier price schedule to sell to different buyers, **price discrimination** exists. Airlines provide a prime example, selling services for the same flight at many different prices depending on the purchase date, age of the buyer, days traveled, and many other factors. Price discrimination is an economic strategy designed to increase economic profitability in a mixed market. It does not mean unfair or illegal manipulation of prices. Sometimes, a **reverse price discrimination** occurs, when a supplier charges the same price to different buyers, although the costs of the supplier to do so differ. One would imagine that price discrimination could only occur if a supplier held a monopoly; however, in a complex economy with so many pricing factors and decisions at work, discrimination in pricing occurs almost everywhere. Sometimes, this variation in prices can help lower prices for consumers, but this is not always the case.

COMMERCIAL AIRLINES

As everyone who purchases tickets on an airline knows, price discrimination is rampant. The same flight from San Francisco to New York may offer a bewildering number of prices based on such factors as:

- Length (number of days) of the trip.
- Age of the traveler.
- Day of the week traveled.
- Purchase date of the ticket.
- Number of stops en route to destination.

- Special fares and discounts not available to all travelers.
- Class of service offered on the flight.
- Flexibility of ticket.

Airlines sell into both business and vacation travel markets and often change their prices significantly. The success of online travel agencies has highlighted the price discrimination for airline tickets. A quick glance at one of these websites will show multiple examples of airline price discrimination.

Adam Smith and Value

Value is the key economic element that drives many business decisions. Unfortunately, **value** may be difficult to define, as it means different things to different people. It is, however, the measurement by which utility, or want-satisfying power, may be defined. Some classical economists, including **Adam Smith**, tied **labor** to value, postulating that true value was the amount of work it takes to produce a good or service for sale. Although this is one legitimate manner in which to measure value, it is not the only one. An exception would be the relative ease of "making" emeralds, compared to the complexity of producing aircraft. The element of **scarcity** is also a vital component of the value of a good or service. Some market theorists claim that **price** itself tells the value of a good or service. They believe that countless economic variables are factored into determining a price for a specific good or service, and this price equals the value. In some sense, value is a determinant of the individual's belief in the want-satisfying power of any good or service.

Competition Policy

Each state has enacted laws designed to control **competition practices** of businesses. These laws cover many aspects of competition but are generally designed to ensure competition is not impeded. They protect small businesses and consumers against the possible abuses of oligopolies and monopolies. Each nation that encourages **free trade** has its own laws to protect competition. However, the adequacy of these laws, and the stringency with which they are enforced, varies widely among countries of the world. Perhaps the United States is most vigilant in these areas, having scores of antitrust laws on the books to protect competition. In America, the **Department of Justice** monitors all proposed mergers and acquisitions to insure they will not significantly reduce competition. They have the power to deny such mergers and takeovers if they feel the public interest is negatively affected. The government has the ability to force large monopolistic conglomerates to break up if they unfairly control markets.

Welfare Economics

The analysis of income distribution and its consequences is called **welfare economics**. This field uses microeconomic theory to measure the effectiveness of the economic system in improving the general welfare. Welfare economics takes as its starting point the individual, the most basic component of an economy. Careful analysis of individual economic behavior yields a much clearer understanding of the macroeconomic picture of an economy. How well the wants and needs of a society are met may be termed **social welfare**. It may be viewed as the aggregate sum of the welfare of all individuals in a society. Welfare can be measured by dollars or income, or more generally in terms of individual economic satisfaction. Two major components of welfare economics are **economic efficiency**, which considers the total wealth of a society, and **income distribution**, which focuses on how the wealth is allocated throughout the economy. Both are key indicators of the general welfare.

Price Elasticity

When a price is changed, there will be a change in the demand for the goods and services. The rate at which demand falls or rises is called the **price elasticity of demand**. This measurement is usually formulated as a ratio of the changing price and the change in demand. If a price is raised by 20% and demand falls by 20%, the ratio between them is the price elasticity of demand. Normally, any rise in price will decrease the demand for the goods and services offered. Any decrease in price should raise demand, barring other external factors. This theory of price elasticity works best as a model, because in the real economic world, there are a huge number of variables that affect price and demand. Usually, businesses will test these variables to determine how much a price change will by itself affects demand.

Cross Elasticity of Demand and Income Elasticity of Demand

If the demand of a good or service is affected by the change in price of a different good or service, **cross elasticity** of demand is at work. This is most often expressed as a ratio between the **change in demand** for the first good as the price of the second good fluctuates. An example of this would be the change in demand for subway tickets in New York if the price of each ticket were to be doubled. The ratio between the drop in demand for use of the subway and the amount of the price increase would be the cross elasticity of demand. The demand for a good or service is related to the income of prospective buyers of the good or service. Changes in the income of prospective consumers are measured in a ratio to the change in demand caused by the income change. If the income of a buyer pool increases 10% and the demand for the product increases 10%, that ratio (1:1) is the income elasticity of demand.

Price Elasticity of Supply

The price of a good or service directly affects the quantity of supply of that good or service. The ratio between the price increase or decrease and the amount of the good or service supplied is called the **price elasticity of supply**. For example, a rise in the price of carrots will cause an increase in the supply of carrots as farmers produce more of that crop to increase profits. This price elasticity of supply is expressed as a ratio between the increase or decrease in price and the increase or decrease of supply. If the price of carrots rises on the open market by 10% and the supply of carrots increases by 10%, the price elasticity of supply would be expressed as the ratio between these changes (1:1). Note that inventories of goods already produced will be a factor in determining the price elasticity of supply. Over the long run, economists equate goods produced with goods supplied.

Surplus

A **consumer surplus** arises when prices fall and buyers realize extra savings, which go into a surplus of buying power for purchasers. If, for any number of economic factors, suppliers are able to sell at higher prices than they would ordinarily obtain, a **supplier surplus** exists. In many areas, particularly commodities and farm products, governments intervene, which may cause an artificial surplus. This government intervention usually takes the form of subsidies of some kind and often represents the government holding a significant surplus itself. Taxes are another area of government intervention that can cause a surplus. When all the existing surpluses in an economy are aggregated, the sum may be called the **total surplus**. Welfare economics uses this figure when they consider a new policy or examine an existing one.

Individual Demand Curves

A demand by consumers or buyers is analyzed based on the ability of any good or service to satisfy the needs of that group. When all economic considerations are in play, including the price of a good or service and the amount supplied, consumers will, in general, choose the economic decisions that most fulfill their wants and needs. When all of these individual preferences are analyzed, the total pattern will represent **aggregate demand curves**. Although each individual will operate to fulfill his or her needs as a separate unit, the aggregate of the total economy may differ. Social programs, tax incentives, and transfer payments will change the pattern of wealth distribution for the entire economy. Society, as an entity, may have a different aggregate demand than any individual. Since there is always a broad spectrum of wants and needs in any given society, the market cannot give a "greatest good for the greatest number" with any certainty.

Theories of Value

Placing value on goods and services has been a problem concerning economists for centuries. Many scholastic and scientific arguments of the reformation period focused on the definition of value. The classical argument of value is illustrated in the "diamond-water paradox." It is pointed out in comparisons of these goods that water is essential to life and either free or available at a low price, while diamonds are a very expensive, unnecessary luxury. Classical economic thinkers claimed that value could only be measured as the cost of production of the product. The difficulty and expense of making a good available imputed it with intrinsic value. Both Adam Smith and David Ricardo promulgated this **theory of value**. Another school of thought on determining value stated that the value of anything was completely subjective; nothing is valuable in and of itself, and only the perceived value imputed by the consumer is valid. This school, called the **subjective theory of value**, asserted itself through the 20th century.

Efficient Market Theory

Capital markets work under a different set of principles than other markets. The market for stocks and bonds is an example of a capital market. Fama's "**efficient market theory**" attempts to describe the forces that operate in capital markets. According to this theory, the price of an equity security or bond is determined by an overall objective assessment of its perceived value after all information regarding the security is available and taken into account. This is only accurate in theory, because it assumes all information about the security is accurate (very rarely true) and that all individuals receive the information at the same time (almost never true). Additional assumptions are made that all relevant information arises spontaneously and the market is broad enough that no small group of individuals can manipulate the price. Sometimes called the "**random walk theory**," it claims that any attempt to forecast market prices based on mathematical calculations or market analysis is futile.

Market Failure

The term *market failure* has several definitions in economics. At the most basic level, it means the market is unable to provide a stable trading framework for the distribution of goods and services to the buyers. In this case, the market does not truly function under the economic definition of a trading exchange. Another way of viewing **market failure** is the common situation where the market is so grossly inefficient it simply malfunctions. Social welfare economists would deem any market that did not place the good of the society above all other factors as a failure. In trying to understand the mechanics of market failure, economists have created models to study the phenomenon. They believe market failure is often the result of errors in pricing based on faulty market research. Inaccurate information in setting prices can be a major cause of failure. Perhaps the major cause of market failure is the failure to adequately understand the nuances of the particular market involved.

Economic Rent

In economics, *economic rent* is a technical term that defines the ratio between the cost of a factor of production and the revenue yielded by that factor. The utilization of each factor of production involves an opportunity cost that must be evaluated by a company. Choices the firm makes will decide on the optimal use of these factors in light of income received. A company must make decisions that select the processes which best optimize the productivity of that firm. A technical distinction may be made between **economic rent** and profits, because business entities often own manufacturing and capital equipment and derive multiple benefits from them. **Profit** is a more narrow concept, which may be calculated easily by subtracting business costs from business income. The two may be substantially different, depending on the organization of a company, ownership of capital goods, and the method of accounting used. Economic rent is a more theoretical term, while profit and loss are practical indicators of the success or failure of a business.

Economies of Scale

Economies of scale is an economic concept that measures the effects of the increase in production of a given product. **Economies of scale** refers to the changing variables that must occur when production is increased or decreased. The goal of this economic measurement is to determine the most ideal size of a company to maximize productivity and decrease inefficiency. Many factors enter into this concept, including the available labor force, size of the physical plant necessary, cost and availability of raw materials, and managerial expertise to mix and balance these elements most effectively. Ultimately, economies of scale are used to increase productivity and profit, the two measurements that are vital to the success of a firm. **Diseconomies of scale** indicate when production changes have reached a point where they are detrimental to the firm. This can be valuable information as companies plan production strategies and levels.

Economies of scope are primarily concerned with the planning and implementation of product mix as a strategy of marketing and distribution. Economies of scale deal with the amounts of goods and services supplied, while economies of scope are more concerned with the types and numbers of different products the firm markets. An example would be a candy manufacturer deciding to introduce a new variation of an existing candy bar. Marketing and distribution channels would remain the same, name recognition would be present, and the product would fit nicely into the overall product concept of the firm. Should the company decide to add shoes to its line, diseconomies of scope become evident. Marketing strategy and distribution agencies would be different, as would packaging, storing, and shipping the final product. Such diseconomies of scope place major barriers in the path of product expansion into new and uncharted markets.

Problems of Oversized Firms

Firms that become too large may encounter problems that impair their efficiency and productivity. The usual result of **oversized firms** is an increase in cost resulting in decreased profits. Several problems are common when a business grows too quickly or reaches an unwieldy size. Many times, rapid growth causes duplication of essential production or marketing functions. Overall communication can slow, with the result of a firm that may be less responsive to changes in the economy or their markets. As firms grow, a certain inertia may set in: an unwillingness to change outmoded business practices. Increased size almost always results in more managers who are further removed from the vital operations of the company. Sometimes, a company will end up competing with itself in some areas. Companies can grow so quickly they lose touch with their customers and fail to accurately assess changing markets. Rapid growth can be desirable but almost always compounds a firm's problems, and often creates new ones.

Top-Heavy Companies

As a company experiences rapid growth, the percentage of middle and upper management usually grows. **Managers** serve a vital function in shaping company policy, supervising operations, and planning for the future. However, managers rarely increase the productivity of a firm. Typically, managers who supervise and do not perform vital company operations will lower the efficiency of an organization. As firms develop over time, managers, who may be viewed as the most unproductive part of the organization, increase in numbers and influence. Sometimes, managers also have dual roles as line workers who directly impact the vital operations of a firm. This is an ideal but uncommon situation. Managers who only supervise add only an intangible and incremental asset to the firm. It is not unusual to see corporations with layers of relatively unproductive **middle and upper management**. This almost always works to the detriment of the company.

Solutions to Outsized Companies

Breaking a large unwieldy company into smaller, more responsive units is often an excellent solution to the **overgrowth** of a company. Firms will sometimes assess their operating divisions and decide to retain only the most profitable ones. Others will be sold or eliminated. Failure of a company that declares bankruptcy sometimes forces such action. Hostile takeovers of a business will almost always result in the elimination of unprofitable centers and the reorganization of the entire company. Government intervention is sometimes the catalyst for the reorganization of a firm that has become too monopolistic. All of these solutions are undesirable when forced upon a company from an outside source. A thoughtful and resourceful firm will take a proactive position in solving **growth problems**. It is much better for a company to position itself to take advantage of growth rather than have changes imposed upon it.

Costs and Revenues

Costs and revenues are the two determinants of income, the most common measuring tools for assessing business success. Firms incur **fixed costs**, which are constant and do not depend on that amount of production. Examples would be physical plants and heavy equipment, which must be paid for even if production is zero. **Variable costs** are tied directly to the production of finished goods and services. As more goods are produced, variable costs rise. Examples of variable costs are raw materials used in the production process, extra labor needed in peak production periods, and additional capital if expansion is needed. **Revenue** is the aggregate amount of income that the firms receive from any source. The most common source of income is the **sale of deeds and services**, but additional monies may be gleaned from transfer payments, investment return, and additional investment by owners. Corporations have the ability to raise money through issuing additional stock or floating bonds at attractive interest rates, as well as using venture capital to increase revenue.

Profit Maximization

The usual goal of any business concern is the **maximization of profits**. Sole business owners, partnerships, and corporations all face this problem. There are a number of common strategies for increasing profits for these concerns. The most important for any type of business is to find the amount of production of finished goods at a certain price that guarantees the best return. One approach is to cut costs to a level to produce an optimum profit. This involves determining at what point the minimum input will result in an optimal level of per-unit products. This would be a level of profit maximization. Another tactic is to increase sales in an attempt to improve the profit picture. A flaw in this approach is that as units produced increase, variable costs also go up. Profit maximization is determined by a myriad of economic factors, some beyond the control of an individual firm. Variables that can be determined by the firm can position it to take advantage of favorable economic conditions. Maximizing opportunities in any economic environment is the challenge for an individual company.

Elements Involved in Pricing

Pricing is an essential element in marketing. It is a sophisticated business practice and one that may cause a product's success or failure. The simple definition of **pricing** is the **assignment of monetary amounts** to goods and services sold by the company. Complexities of this process include varying prices to different customers, special price promotions, determining the price based on fluctuating variable costs, special quantity pricing, incentive pricing for multiple orders of dissimilar products, and accurately assessing the price the market will bear. Pricing must be based on accurate market research, which provides insights into the buying habits of the potential market. Clear objectives for pricing must be set, and knowledge of the competition's pricing policies is critical. Decisions must be made on volume or bulk pricing, pricing for international sales, zone pricing (varying prices in different geographical areas), the use of discounts, and the understanding of the market's price sensitivity. All of those factors (and several others) will determine the price charged for a particular good or service.

Process of Setting Goals in Pricing

Prices are determined to fulfill several purposes, the main one being a sufficient price to ensure sales that will attain the **financial goals** of the firm. The price must also be realistic when compared to the marketplace and competition. It would be an error to price a new candy bar at $1.00 if competing bars of similar size sell for $0.75. Price must also fit into a company's overall marketing plan, which will include channels of distribution, manufacturing requirements, and storing and shipping facilities. The quality of the product in the market (high-end/low-end), planned promotional and overall marketing strategies, and the effectiveness of the sales force all play a part in pricing. In general, prices should reflect the most that customers are willing to pay for it. This will usually result in the most income per unit. The **effective price** of a product is monies the firm obtains from sales of goods and services after special pricing strategies (promotions, incentives, and discounts) are considered.

Special Pricing Strategies

There are several special pricing strategies used in different phases of the life of the product. When a product is introduced, an introductory lower price may induce people to try the product. The goal is to secure a market base and then raise the price to a more appropriate level. Sometimes a price is applied that is near the highest level of the pricing scale. This is intended to underscore the quality of the product and is sometimes called premium pricing. Retailers sometimes use artificially lower prices on some products to attract customers in the hope they will make additional purchases. This is called **"loss leader" pricing**. **Demand pricing** is any pricing tactic that is based on market research into consumer demand for the product. Consumers tend to believe a higher price (within reason) relates to a higher-quality product. Products may be sold together (bundled) at a special price. Economies of scope, scale, and agglomeration all play an important role in **special pricing strategies**.

Perfect Competition and Monopolistic Competition

There is no such thing as perfect competition in the real world. It exists only as an economic model, describing a theoretical market where the base of producers and consumers is so large that they are unable to influence prices. Ideally, this would lead to a textbook definition of economic efficiency. For **perfect competition** to exist, products are essentially the same, each type being an equal substitute for another. Prices are set by the market, and firms must accept this determination.

All businesses must have equal access to existing information, raw materials, and the latest technology. **Monopolistic competition** has a different set of standards. Usually, there are numerous producers and a great number of consumers in any market. No regulations exist to entering or leaving the market, and consumers have more product knowledge and have definite choices between products. These markets give individual companies more influence over their markets. They may raise or lower prices and make adjustments based on the response of the market.

OLIGOPOLY AND OLIGOPSONY

When any particular market is controlled by a small group of suppliers, an **oligopoly** is said to exist. In this situation, all suppliers are cognizant of each other's activities. When any one firm makes an economic decision, it will impact the activity of all other firms in the oligopoly. There is a great deal of interaction between members of oligopolies, and planning by any one firm must consider the likely responses of all other members. Oligopolies were very common in certain industries, but antitrust laws have limited their power. In an **oligopsony** market, there are limited numbers of buyers and an unlimited number of sellers. When a relatively small number of businesses are competing to acquire factors of production, this situation is common. Here, buyers will have a competitive advantage and will be aware of each other's economic activity. Sometimes, a situation arises where there are only a few buyers and a few sellers. This unusual situation results in a **bilateral oligopsony**.

MONOPOLY AND MONOPSONY

When one supplier is the sole seller of a service or product, a **monopoly** is said to exist. There is no competition in a monopolistic economy, as there is only one provider or seller. Usually, in a monopoly, there are no ready substitutes for the products being supplied. Some monopolies are legal in a sense, a prime example being AT&T before it was broken up by government intervention. **Legal monopolies** are common in government agencies and institutions and sometimes exist in specialized private sectors of the economy. Sometimes, an economic phenomenon occurs where there is only a single consumer of a product, and there may be a number of suppliers. This is called **monopsony** and only occurs in specialized industries that have large institutional consumers. **Cartels** differ from monopolies by coordinating the action of a few suppliers to gain economic advantage. Cartels are several firms acting in concert to create an economic advantage. Cartels organize and act as if one business in order to control a finite market.

MONOPOLISTIC COMPETITION, HORIZONTAL MONOPOLY, AND VERTICAL MONOPOLY

When an industry or portion of an industry is so dominated by a company that it controls the market completely, a **"de facto" monopoly** is said to exist. This condition is sometimes called **monopolistic competition**. The dominance of Microsoft in computer software in the 1980s and '90s created monopolistic competition. The government has intervened at a few points in the past. Sometimes, a large corporation will buy or control smaller firms who are considered competitors and create a **horizontal monopoly**. These companies may have different names and trademarks but still belong to the parent corporation. This type of economic organization is called a horizontal monopoly. A **vertical monopoly** is the control of associated goods and services by one corporation. For example, an oil company may own oil fields, refineries, and distribution channels to retailers in order to control an entire production and marketing flow for a product.

CHARACTERISTICS OF A MONOPOLY

To qualify as a monopoly, several conditions must exist. Primarily, there is only **one producer or supplier** of a good or service, and attempts for other firms to enter as competitors are discouraged by economic action of the monopoly holder. This action may be based on better or unique technology, patents on products that allow no competition, and the economic realities of trying to enter a market that is controlled by such a dominating economic entity. These actions and others like them are collectively called **blocking the entry** to a monopolistic market. These economic actions may or may not be in restraint of trade. In a monopolistic situation, the product being monopolized usually has **no comparable substitutes or alternatives**. It can have no true competition, forcing consumers to buy from the monopolizing corporation. The company controlling the monopoly can manipulate the price and available supply of the product involved. Artificial shortages can be created that force prices upward.

Business Organizations

Business organizations operate under a bevy of laws and regulations that mandate both their organization and activities. There are a number of types of organization that companies may choose. The most common form of business entity is the **sole proprietorship**. An example of this would be "mom and pop" businesses found everywhere. **Partnerships** bring together two or more individuals as joint owners of a business. There are a number of various types of partnerships that define, limit, and regulate business practices and liabilities. Most familiar is the **corporate** form of business organization. Many familiar United States companies are organized and run as corporations. Besides these more common forms of organization, specialized types of arrangements such as limited liability companies, cooperatives formed by individuals for specific economic purposes, government-owned institutions, and pension funds and credit unions may be found in most economies.

Sole Proprietorship

A privately owned business with one principal owner who operates in his or her own name is called a **sole proprietorship**. Such an organization essentially functions as an individual who incurs any debts or liabilities of the business as personal obligations. For example, a lawsuit against a sole proprietorship that gains a judgment could seek compensation from both the business and the individual. Taxation affects the sole proprietorship much like an individual, in that he or she is taxed on personal and business income. Requirements for accounting and regulations are much simpler for the sole proprietorship type of organization. Individuals owning small businesses may still choose to name their business as they wish and can file for a registered trade name that allows them to do business under that name rather than their own. Even in these cases, the individual remains responsible for the debts and liabilities of his or her business.

Partnerships

Partnerships are business organizations where two or more individuals enter into an agreement to share in the financial proceeds (or losses) of a business in which they have invested resources. **General partners** are fully responsible for all liabilities the partnership incurs to third parties. **Limited partners**, while still liable for debts and obligations of the partnership, have their exposure limited to the extent they are invested in the organization. **Silent partners** are those who take no active role in operating the business, and may or may not be publicly associated with the firm. Partnerships often involve the legal formality of declaring their intention to do business. A formal agreement of partnership may be prepared and a public announcement made of the formation of the partnership, with some jurisdictions requiring partnerships to register and make available their records to the public. These usually include only the terms of the partnership and not financial records.

Limited Partnerships and Limited Liability Partnerships

Generally, a limited partnership operates under the same conditions as a general partnership, with the exception that one or more limited partners join one or more general partners in the organization. **General partners** have all the rights and liabilities of any business owner. **Limited partners** initially make a specific investment of funds to the partnership, and their liability for debts and judgments against the partnership is limited to the amount of their investment. Limited partners have no role in managing the operations of the partnership, except in an advisory capacity. They are, however, required to publicly declare their ownership by various registration procedures. Organizations of professionals, such as physicians, attorneys, and other such groups, often form **Limited Liability Partnerships**, which place various limits on the financial exposure of each partner. Limits and statutes vary between states, but often, partners are protected from liability in a judgment simply because they belong to the organization.

CORPORATIONS

The term *corporation* is a legal one, defining the rules and regulations for a business, non-profit organization, or institution to **incorporate**. Governmental entities such as cities and towns may also choose to incorporate. Voluntary associations need not apply for corporate status. **Corporations** often operate as an **individual person** might, with power to make agreements, own land and capital equipment, and participate in business. In a sense, a corporation is a person under the law, and subject to rules and regulations any person must abide by. Additionally, there are specific obligations a corporation must perform, including public registration and other regulations deemed necessary by the state in which the corporation intends to do business. Corporations differ from individuals in some important ways. They cannot cast votes in public elections, nor can they as an entity be imprisoned (although individual members of the corporation could be incarcerated).

FEATURES

Corporations must file formal documents with a state describing the particulars of the **intended corporation**. This includes any stock issues (public or private), the identity of officers of the proposed corporation, and the general rules and operating procedures for the corporation. The laws of the state in which the corporation is licensed regulate its business practices, including many financial restrictions. When stock is issued, shareholders of a corporation may be individuals, institutions, other corporations, or government agencies. If no stock is involved in the corporation, it may still incorporate and often is called a "society," "membership corporation," or other title indicating no stock is outstanding for the corporation. There is usually a board of officers and directors who operate the corporation on behalf of the owners. This board is responsible for the financial affairs of the company, as well as making policy and human resource decisions, including the appointment or election of the major officers of the firm.

TYPES

When the term corporation is used to describe a business organization, what immediately comes to mind is a business that issues common or preferred stock that is publicly traded on an organized stock exchange. More accurately, this type of business organization is called a **public corporation**. Many large and familiar firms fall into this category. Privately held corporations, known as **closed corporations**, are much more common. These entities may issue stock to a select number of officers, but there is no public trading on any organized market. Both individuals and companies may be the stockholders of these closed corporations. They usually include only a relatively small number of stockholders. Some corporations have expanded (or were originally organized) to do business all over the world. The phenomenon of globalization has witnessed the increasing number and economic power of what we now term *multinational corporations*. These companies are regulated in each country in which they do business. Some are separately incorporated in multiple countries.

Economic Theory of Pareto Efficiency

An important economic theory that studies the effects of alternative choices in resource allocation is **Pareto efficiency**. This is an important analytical tool in modern economics. First posited by the Italian economist **Vilfredo Pareto**, it seeks to study the level of economic efficiency determined by the distribution of income. Simply stated, if a change in the allocation of resources improves the economic condition of one individual or group without hurting another individual or group, this is called **Pareto improvement**. Pareto efficiency is a sophisticated economic analytical tool that incorporates aspects of mathematics, social science, and engineering. If an economy is proved to be Pareto efficient, then no individual or group within that economy can be improved by switching allocations of resources without degrading the economic condition of another individual or group in that economy. In this case, no shift of resources will benefit the society.

Abram Bergson's Social Welfare Function

An economic tool that measures the economic welfare of a given society after considering all relevant economic factors is called the **social welfare function**. There are a number of possible standards for measuring the social welfare of an economy, including financial, social, and political elements. First introduced by the economist **Abram Bergson** in the 1930s, social welfare was posited to be the aggregate level of want-satisfying attainment by all individuals in a society. In a sense, social welfare reflects the values and goals of a society. In the United States, for example, a social and economic goal is to make retired and older citizens who cannot work economically better off. To achieve this social and economic objective, the government has introduced transfer payment programs over the years, primarily through social security. Another objective is to provide those unable to work with sufficient income to be economically viable. Unemployment and disability transfer payments by state and federal governments seek to attain this.

Lorenz Curve

One of the most useful indicators of equality and inequality in income distribution in an economy is the **Lorenz curve**. Developed in the early 20th century by **Max Lorenz**, it paints a graphical representation of the **distribution of income** in a society. The Lorenz curve first posits a state of perfect income equality and compares actual income distribution with the ideal. Another use of the Lorenz curve is to plot the patterns of asset distribution in an economy. The Lorenz curve can indicate what percentage of total income certain economic individuals or households hold. This is done by creating a graph of the curve, with each point measuring relative income. For example, we may learn that 70% of the total income of an economy is held by 30% of the households. The Lorenz curve provides a schedule that charts these ratios. The Lorenz curve and other such relative indicators of income distribution are sometimes used in welfare economics to measure the equality of the economic system. Many social programs are based on these analyses.

Externality in Economic Decisions

When an economic decision made by a person who has no economic gain or loss at stake results in a significant impact on others, it is said to be an **externality**. This occurs when the decision-maker is in a neutral position regarding any gains and losses from the decision. The catalyst for the decision makes economic choices that affect others with no risk. Governments often make such decisions that have an important impact on others but not on the individual who makes the choice. Examples of externalities would be the permission to drill for oil on a nature preserve. The decision may be made in Washington by a government official who has no financial interest in petroleum and does not live near the natural habitat. Yet the decision will have far-reaching effects on a large group of suppliers and consumers. Externalities may usually be traced back to a demand and supply situation. An increased need for oil may have determined the decision for oil exploration in a natural habitat.

Free Goods

In economic analysis, a free good is used rather loosely to designate a good or service that is abundant. This means such goods are available to everyone at little or no cost to the economy. Examples of **free goods** include natural resources owned by the public, water, and air. Some free goods are so easily available that everyone can have as much as they want under ordinary circumstances. Other free goods may be the result of cooperation between economic entities, including governments, to yield an excess of a good for the general welfare. Some free goods are intangible. Examples would include the skies used by airlines, the oceans used to fish and dredge for assets, and ideas or inventions that fall into the public domain. A modern economic intangible is the creation of internet technology, which is a complex combination of ideas, cutting-edge technology, and public access. No one owns the internet, yet is used for a myriad of economic (and personal) purposes.

Tragedy of the Commons

In the constant competition for resources between components of an economy, there arises a phenomenon called "**the tragedy of the commons**." This controversy begs the question as to the ownership of natural resources such as the seas and atmosphere. Can individuals claim as their own the vast resources of the planet, or do they belong to everyone? Should these resources be used for individual gain, or to promote the general welfare? These are the questions raised by the tragedy of the commons, a term coined by **Garrett Hardin**. The concept has been expanded in contemporary economics to describe perceived selfish behavior in all living things. The drive for survival and dominance in nature as well as economics provides many examples of the primacy of **self-interest**. From this self-interest and its results, the **common good** often suffers because of individual actions. This is the larger meaning of the tragedy of the commons.

Modern Examples

Contemporary examples of the tragedy of the commons are evident in all aspects of society. Pollution in all its forms, including air pollution and water pollution, are prime examples of the tragedy of the commons. The irresponsible consumption of logging in forests, depletion of the ocean's resources by over-harvesting and pollution, the indiscriminate littering and graffiti common in cities, and traffic congestion (causing additional pollution and lowered quality of life) are all part of the tragedy of the commons. The less obvious but still destructive examples are noise pollution, legalized gambling, and the seamier sides of the internet, including pornography and massive spamming. These all have negative impacts on the quality of life because of the selfish action of special groups and interests. Whenever there is a degrading of the general welfare in any manner by a small percentage of the population, the tragedy of the commons is seen.

Tragedy of the Anticommons

When there is a collective or individual activity that results in an **under-use** of a scarce resource, this is the **tragedy of the anticommons**. This is contrasted with the tragedy of the commons, which is an overuse or misuse of a scarce resource, which negatively affects the general welfare. If a resource is ignored or underutilized by large numbers of individuals, a different type of waste occurs. This situation is common when a large segment of the economic society is excluded by some means from access to the resource. Common contemporary examples are found in biomedical and pharmacological research, where patents prevent the cooperative development of therapeutic drugs and technology. Property rights are often cited as an example of tragedy of the anticommons, as they exclude a large number of individuals from fully participating in the economic system. When a large part of society is denied access to a fundamental economic activity, that activity may be said to be under-used because the resource is available only to a relative few.

Efficient Market Theory

The mechanisms and activity of capital markets are explained by **efficient market theory**. Using the price of an equity as an example, the price of a stock or bond is a result of all known information and news about the equity and market. This total information results in a rational estimation of the true intrinsic value of the equity. Such a price will have accounted for all positive and negative information of the equity. The price may be said to be **discounted** or **adjusted** for all known information. Should anyone have special access to such information, they are in a position of competitive advantage relative to the equity. This theory makes certain assumptions about the market. These include a large market with many individuals trading for the equity, the presence of perfect information about the stock and market, and free and equal access to all information. Market news is assumed to rise randomly and be available to all at the same time. Efficient market theory is rarely seen in the real world, because the necessary conditions for such a condition to exist almost never occur.

Financial Economics

The branch of economics that deals with business finance, including financing individual firms and corporations, is called **financial economics**. This field also encompasses the financial markets, commodity exchanges, and money markets. Financial economics is governed by several basic principles:

- **Risk or uncertainty** - the gain or loss of monetary assets is not presently known, but will be determined in the future by economic determinants.
- **The element of time** - the monetary gain or loss changes over time.
- **Economic options** - any party to an economic exchange is free to make a decision that will affect future results.
- **Economic information** - economic information can alter future economic activity, result in monetary gains and losses, and change the dynamics of the participants.

Financial economics considers the determinants of prices of financial assets, alternatives for business financing, and personal business decisions that result in reaching economic objectives.

Time Value of Money

A basic precept of business finance is the **time value of money**. Known also as the discounted present value of money, this principle is crucial in decision-making in business finance. Stated simply, the time value of money means an individual would rather have his or her money now than in the future. If the possession of the money is deferred, a price is paid for the delay. This price reflects the time value of money. For example, if $10 today will accrue to $12 in one year, the time value of money for that period is $2. The time value of money is about **future risk**. The value of money today might be worth more or less in the future, depending on inflation or deflation. An investor or lender (or borrower) gives up a certain value today for an uncertain value sometime in the future. Astute individuals will evaluate economic conditions with a view toward predicting the future value of money and base their economic decisions on that projection.

Business Finance

Corporate or managerial finance is the process of acquiring and using funds for business operations. This requires an assessment of potential risk and opportunity for the utilization of monies. Decisions regarding the capital structure of a firm, either by equity financing or the issuing of bonds, must be made. The monies necessary for operations, or working capital, may be provided by income from operations or by a line of credit from a lending institution. Firms may choose to issue bonds to finance operations. The company may then sell the bonds, which carry an interest rate, to investors. These bonds may be traded on the open market, and the price will fluctuate with interest rates. Financial managers of companies may choose to use profits to invest in an array of possible investments, each positioned for a different strategy. The financial function of businesses is critical for their success, both in the shortterm and over a long period. Strategies vary according to the overall position of the firm, its industry goals, and the financial health of the firm.

Risk

Risk is the possible negative effect a business activity or decision carries. **Risk assessment** includes both the probability of a negative event and the assessment of the impact of the potential event. Risk varies from industry to industry and can be applied to a variety of business (or individual) decisions. Risks are an inevitable part of business, and the object of a firm is to minimize risk and maximize return. **Business risks** include marketing decisions, financial choices, production and product delivery systems, and a myriad of other business functions. **Financial risks** are considered to be excellent testing grounds for other business decisions. Current thinking in risk appraisal involves predicting the level of exposure and vulnerability if the potential risk is realized. Managers ask themselves what results they would be willing to live with should the risk become an event. This assessment includes a multitude of factors that must be considered, depending on the nature and possible impact of the risk in question.

General Equilibrium Theory

General equilibrium theory provides a picture of the entire economy, beginning with individuals and their markets. An important part of microeconomics, it models an infinite number of markets for goods and services, beginning with the most basic units in the economy. In this manner, it portrays the entire economy as a sum of all its individual units. It differs from macroeconomics, which begins its analysis of the economy using aggregate numbers. **Modern general equilibrium theory** is a highly sophisticated tool and requires the use of computer technology to generate its models. The vast numbers of individuals and markets included in such an analysis would not have been possible until the widespread use of computers in economic analysis. Generating economic aggregates from individual transactions allows economists to build a model of the economy with a degree of accuracy. It answers the question of how macroeconomics obtains its data. A relatively new tool of economists, the general equilibrium theory promises both comprehensive and accurate raw material with which to build a model of the entire economy.

Neoclassical Economics in Depth

Neoclassical economics is founded on certain assumptions about economic activities. Based on the theories of supply and demand, it assumes all economic units are making rational decisions. Each unit will attempt to maximize their gain or individual economic satisfaction through these decisions, which are based on the economic information available to them. **Neoclassical economics** is, to a large degree, what we call **mainstream economic theory**. Critics of neoclassical economics have been effective in showing obvious flaws in many of the assumptions of the school. These criticisms have often evolved into new schools of economic thought, seeking to find a more realistic way of understanding economic decisions and their results. The very definition of what constitutes neoclassical economics is an area of debate, as neoclassical economists have a wide variety of approaches and analyses for most economic problems. The areas of disagreement from within neoclassical economics and from those who challenge the basic premises of the field have caused a degree of confusion in economic study. It is safe to say that neoclassical economics is in a state of relative flux as new and revised thinking is brought to economic analysis.

AUSTRIAN SCHOOL OF ECONOMICS AND CARL MENGER

The 20th century saw the birth of the **Austrian school of economics**, a hybrid school that stands outside the traditional schools of mainstream economic theory. Perhaps the most important proponent of the Austrian school is **Carl Menger**, who, with his associates and colleagues, pioneered the economic theory upon which the Austrian school was founded. **Anti-Keynesian** in approach, the Austrian school has rejected the bioeconomic model of imposing the principles of life sciences to the subject of economics. Employing a logical and intuitive set of tools collectively called **praxeology**, the Austrian school takes a more formal approach to economic theory. The success of the Austrian school has been influential by focusing on the generative stage of economic productivity. It has successfully challenged the behavioral basis of economic theory, in favor of more traditional formal aspects of cause and effect in economic theory. Groups or political associations that profess a libertarian or liberal philosophy view the Austrian school favorably and share many of their social and political goals.

BEHAVIORAL ECONOMICS

Behavioral economics draws heavily from a number of social sciences and related fields to attempt to understand the behaviors and emotional components of economic activities. Working with the traditional economic framework of allocation of scarce resources, supply, demand, and pricing policy, **behavioral economics** inquires of the reasoning and motivation for economic choices. Behavioral economists study the rational behavior of economic entities and attempt to predict results based on these rational decisions. Behavioral economics posits "**heuristics**," that decision making is often intuitive or behavioral rather than strictly rational. It believes that the way an economic choice is presented to a firm or individual will determine its ultimate decision. Behavioral economics also tackles the phenomena of market inefficiencies, explaining why the behavior of markets often defy logical and expected outcomes.

CRITICISMS

Opponents of **behavioral economics** often base their arguments on the rational activities of an economy and its units. They contend that the behaviorists ignore market realities, particularly the ability of economic units to learn, modify their choices, and improve their opportunities for success. They feel these factors will move all players in the market toward rational decision-making, upon which neoclassical economics is built. They also claim that cognitive theories do not reflect general economic activity but rather focus on a narrow area of decision-making. Thus, decision-making using a cognitive model cannot be validly imposed on economic decisions. Behavioral economics relies upon surveys and questionnaires to obtain data on economic choices. Critics feel these tools are often poorly constructed and fail to consider that revealed preferences are more accurate in predicting economic behavior than responses from surveys. Bias and subjectivity are sometimes incorporated into the research tools of behavioral economics, making them suspect.

ECOLOGICAL ECONOMICS

The increasing importance of ecology in the last half of the 20th century gave rise to the innovative field of **ecological economics**. This branch of economics concerns itself with the relationships between economics and extant ecosystems in the biosphere. It has common elements with the "green" movement and incorporates human development theory into its approach to economics. The major goal of ecological economics is to protect and preserve resources through **sustainable development** of those resources. Sustainable development means that the resource in question will not be exploited and destroyed by irresponsible economic activity. Ecological economics positions itself as a subdivision of ecology, maintaining that economics is inherent in the interaction of ecosystems in the biosphere. It tends to place an increased importance on the use and misuse of natural resources, which are seen to be the most important of the factors of production.

PROFIT

The word *profit* is derived from the Latin word *proficere*, whichmeans "to go forward or advance." In an economic sense, **profit** is the gain made from an economic transaction made by a business or individual. Profit may be defined in a multitude of ways, depending on the economic system and the method of accounting within that system. In **investment transactions**, profit is understood to be the return over time of an input of land, labor, and capital. In **business concerns**, this is usually expressed as a rate of return for the assets utilized. Most business concerns measure profit as the difference between revenue received and costs. Economists broaden this definition to include the return from an economic action when the opportunity costs of all other possible choices are considered. The drive for businesses to maximize profits is considered a stimulus to economic activity. It provides motivation and actual rewards for astute economic decisions.

BUSINESS COMPETITION

Competition is the driving force that is the lifeblood of capitalism. It tends to motivate innovations and promotes efficient use of resources and profits. Microeconomic theory holds that **competition** is the most important factor in determining resource allocation. Competition forces companies to develop new products and improve existing ones. It spurs technology, refines production capability, and thus provides consumers with an abundance of superior products and services. Competition tends to stabilize prices and insures no one major supplier can dominate an industry. Competition may find two products competing head-to-head in direct competition. Sometimes, firms develop similar products that may be used instead of existing ones, an example of **substitute competition**. Most competition is seen in pricing, production costs, product mixes, marketing, channels of distribution, and consumer satisfaction. These elements fall under the umbrella of **budget competition**.

WAGE DETERMINATION

The value of **real wages** can only be accurately measured when the productivity of labor is known. Real wages rise when increased levels of technology and per capita investment in labor occurs. The totality of all firms' demand for labor is called the **total market demand for labor**. The market supply of labor depends on the population, level of skill required, prevalent economic condition, and effective wage rate. When the demand and supply curves for labor intersect, the **competitive equilibrium wage rate** is determined. Firms will continue to hire labor until the marginal revenue product of labor, or its demand for labor, reaches the wage rate. **Labor unions** can distort the supply and demand for labor, and thus the wage determination, by increasing productivity, reducing the labor force with excessive union dues, and bargaining with businesses and threatening strikes. All of these activities enter into the determination of wages.

RENT AND INTEREST

Land and other natural resources are limited in supply and thus scarce in economic terms. The price of using land and associated resources is called **rent**. Pricing rent differs from other factors of production, as the total amount of land is fixed. The market demand and price of rent paid do not change the amount of land available for use. **Interest** may be expressed as the price of using money over a period of time, usually expressed in a percentage ratio. Interest rates vary, often to a large degree, depending on the competitive environment, the amount of risk in the loan, the length of the loan, and associated administrative costs involved with the loan. Demand for funds comes from individuals, businesses, and governments. The supply of money available for loan is the accrued aggregate savings of businesses and individuals. This supply is largely determined by the money supply available, which in turn is affected by the monetary policies of the government.

Theory of Games and Economic Behavior, Handbook of Econometrics, and The Handbook of Experimental Economics.

1. *Theory of Games and Economic Behavior* - John Von Neumann and Oskar Morgenstern

Description: A book by the mathematician John von Neumann and economist Oskar Morgenstern. It contains a mathematical theory of economic and social organization, based on a theory of games of strategy. This is now a classic work, upon which modern-day game theory is based.

2. *Handbook of Econometrics* - Zvi Griliches and M. D. Intriligator (eds.)

Description: a five-volume work that is the definitive study of econometrics.

3. *The Handbook of Experimental Economics* – J. H. Kagel and A. E. Roth (eds.)

Description: the most influential experimental economics handbook.

Some of the most important new theories and concepts in microeconomics are published in academic journals such as the *Journal of Econometrics*, *Journal of the American Statistical Society*, and the *Journal of Monetary Economics*. A number of professional business journals offer excellent material.

Poverty Line

The term *poverty line* is commonly used in assessing the success or failure of an economic system. A level of income that fails to reach the minimum for people to purchase the necessities of life is the **poverty line**. Individuals or households falling below this line are unable to provide for themselves and have zero disposable income. Of course, a key consideration is where to draw the poverty line on the economic scale. Because of different prices, costs of living, and varied wage scales, poverty lines are different for each country. When comparing poverty lines between countries, the accepted standard is the **purchasing power exchange rate**. This reveals the relative ability between countries to buy, say, a loaf of bread. Poverty exists to some degree in almost all economic systems. The line is an excellent tool to measure the number and percent of those living in poverty and may form the basis of remedial social programs.

Large Market Share and Public and Government Opposition

As companies grow, it becomes more difficult to increase **market share** regularly. They may diversify into related industries but at the cost of some economies of scope and scale. If a firm grows too large and becomes too successful, it may attract negative publicity and even the attention of the government's **regulatory agencies**. Microsoft is an example of a firm whose dominance attracted unwelcome intervention from external sources. Walmart is another successful corporation that has faced negative publicity and public scrutiny. While these are extreme examples, they occur with some frequency in the corporate world. Larger companies tend to be those who have been in business for a long time and are set on older policies that may not apply to current business conditions. They incur additional fixed costs from pension funds, company benefits, and time lost through sickness. They often control larger portions of the market, making percentage growth more difficult each year. Labor costs may include meeting union demands and the possibility of strikes or work stoppages.

Suggested Retail Price and MSRP

Manufacturers will often make a recommendation as to the **retail price** of a product. This is usually an effort to ensure that the product is sold at a similar price in various locations. Retailers take different approaches to these suggested prices. Some will adhere to the suggested price, while others will discount the price and feature the reduced price as a promotion. Retailers may use their size and/or market position to price goods significantly cheaper than more poorly positioned retailers. An example of this is the price comparisons on almost all unregulated goods between discount houses, convenience stores, and normal retail outlets. Often, prices are set based on the wholesale prices charged to the retailers by suppliers.

Fair trade laws were enacted to protect small retailers from unfair competition from discount houses and chain retail operations. These laws were deemed to be illegal, as they restrained free trade. Manufacturers responded with the **Manufacturers Suggested Retail Price (MSRP)**, which only provides guidelines for retailers. Usually, the MSRP is heavily discounted in order to suggest a product is an excellent bargain at that price.

Revealed Preference Theory

Predicting the buying patterns by consumers can be measured by the **revealed preference theory**, first articulated by **Paul Samuelson**, author of a best-selling economics textbook and a leading figure in contemporary economics. Samuelson postulated that past buying habits could be used to analyze and predict future consumer activity. Samuelson posited that if a consumer purchases a certain brand of ice cream, he or she will continue to do so until something changes his or her mind. Such a change might involve ice cream prices, better-quality ice cream available from a competitor, discontinuation of a favorite flavor or brand, or a host of other conscious and unconscious variables. The consumer may decide to lose weight and give up ice cream as a staple of his or her diet. It can readily be seen that determining these consumer preferences is difficult since it is impossible to know all the factors involved in consumer decisions. Even so, revealed preference theory provides a base from which economists can study purchasing habits of individuals.

Indifference Curves

Indifference curves are another example of a microeconomic tool that measures consumer activity. **Indifference curves** graphically display points on a spectrum where consumers are indifferent to a choice between two products. An indifference curve showing an individual's preference for, say, shirts, might indicate that the desire for a polo shirt and a turtleneck shirt was identical. Thus, both the polo and turtleneck shirts would all be located on the same point of the indifference curve. Indifference curves were introduced as microeconomic tools by economists early in the 20th century. It stemmed from the understanding that consumer satisfaction could be accurately measured. This was called "**cardinal utility**." The new concept uses the principle of "**ordinal utility**," relying on individual economic decisions that could be objectively observed, analyzed, contrasted, and compared, to become the basis for future predictions. From this graphical presentation of data, economists hope to better understand past consumption patterns and future buying activity.

Utility

Utility is a technical economic term that seeks to measure the want-satisfying power of goods and services purchased by consumers. Everyone rationally attempts to increase their **utility**, that is to say, increase their satisfaction gained by economic choices. All goods and services may be measured on an economic scale that rates the utility of that product. Consumer choices (and all microeconomic choices) are made to increase overall utility for that entity. Some goods and services have **increasing utility**, the ability to better satisfy the individual's needs. Others have

decreasing utility, less effective as want-satisfying products. Utility is combined with other economic tools such as indifference curves to attempt to measure and predict consumer behavior. Utility is also an important feature of welfare economics, where it is used to attempt to create the most satisfaction for the most people in an economy. The concept of utility as an economic tool was pioneered by Jeremy Bentham in the 17th century as an aspect of political economy.

Cardinal and Ordinal Utility

Economists have striven for centuries to improve the economic position of society as a whole. This goal spurred economists to attempt to **measure utility** in a meaningful way in order to maximize it for society. If utility could be measured for an individual, it was postulated that the aggregate utility for society could also be measured. This was called **cardinal utility**. The problem with attempting to measure cardinal utility is the difficulty of measuring utility without an objective means of analyzing the information. Each individual has a different set of needs and wants, and comparing a product's utility between diverse groups is impossible. Cardinal utility was abandoned as a useful tool in economics and replaced by the concept of ordinal utility. **Ordinal utility** applied the scientific method to utility by observing patterns of prior economic behavior, comparing economic variables, and postulating predictions of future activity. This has proved to be a more valuable approach in economic analysis.

Income

Income is the compensation received by economic units during the normal activities of business. This includes monies received from multiple sources, including employers, investments, and gifts. In the business world, **gross income** is the amount a company earns before expenses. **Net income** is the money the company has earned after paying the costs of doing business. A company's revenue flow starts with monies received from goods and services sold to consumers. From this amount must be subtracted all monies spent in the operations of the business. This includes employee salaries, costs of production, fixed and variable costs of doing business, and any intangible costs. The resulting figure is the firm's **income** (or loss). If a profit is made, this may be paid as additional compensation to owners, appropriate tax levies, or reinvested to improve the company's position in some respect. Publicly held corporations may choose to pay their stockholders a dividend.

Per Capita Income and Personal Income

The calculation of per capita income is made by taking the total of all monies earned by residents of a particular area divided by the number of inhabitants of the region. Note that **per capita income** is based on where the individuals live, rather than where they physically work. The aggregate of all monies, including passive income, is called **total personal income**. This figure includes all earnings paid to individuals, transfer payments (social security for example), and investment income from all sources. The relative economic health of a particular area can be measured in part by per capita income and total personal income. **Passive income** is also accounted for in total personal income. These are monies derived from rents, private portfolios of stocks and bonds, earned interest from any source, and various payments from pension funds and other employee retirement programs. Another class of income is derived from **government transfer payments**. These include various social and disability benefits, as well as compensation for the unemployed.

Information Asymmetry

In any economic transaction, a party with superior information commands a great advantage. When this is the case, **information asymmetry** is said to exist. An example would be the seller of a home knowing certain structural weaknesses that the buyer does not know. Frequently, **sellers** have more information because they are privy to details about their own property. Occasionally, **buyers** may have the advantage in knowledge. Information asymmetry allows dishonest sellers to sell inferior or substandard products to buyers who are unaware of the information. In a market with broad information asymmetry, the value of all products in the market, good and bad, may decline because of the lack of trust by buyers. If the situation is too commonplace, the market will fail. Knowledgeable consumers will no longer be willing to participate in such an unfair market.

Economies of Agglomeration

There are important benefits to be gained when companies follow a strategy of locating themselves physically close to each other. This strategy and the benefits it yields are called **economies of agglomeration**. Most commonly used in urban areas where multiple similar firms operate, economies of agglomeration is useful in various ways. It provides for a network effect valuable in efficiency in receiving raw materials, drawing from experienced labor pools, and creating competitive advantages in many ways. This is true whether the companies grouped together are complementary or competitive. Both suppliers of raw materials and potential buyers will find it more convenient to work with companies that are physically near each other. Some areas, such as Silicone Valley, are associated with particular industries. **Diseconomies of agglomeration** also exist when firms group close together. Buyers may shop competitively more easily in a small geographic area. Numerous plants and manufacturing operations can degrade the quality of life in an area. A balance of these factors usually occurs in most modern urban areas.

Income Inequality Distribution Measurement

The measurement of income distribution in an economy is done by a set of analytical tools collectively called **income distribution metrics**. The overall purpose of this analysis is to identify patterns of wealth in a society and determine the fairness or inequality of the economy. One set of techniques sets a standard for income and then determines the number of individuals who fall below that line. This approach is most effective in measuring the degree of poverty in a given economy. Examples of these tools in the United States include the poverty line and the number of people living below it. Another group of tools compares income levels between groups and individuals in order to determine how income is distributed in a society and locate patterns of inequality. There are a number of these types of analytical techniques, with the relative poverty line and the Lorenz curve being the best known.

Poverty Lines

The development of poverty lines is an issue each economy faces as it develops social and economic policy. Some countries use a base figure and adjust it for inflation and deflation. The criteria used to determine the fixed figure can vary between countries to a large degree. Comparing **poverty lines** among countries is a complex and sometimes frustrating problem, as prices, wages, and standards fluctuate over time. For example, the European Common Market first computes the median household income and then arbitrarily sets the poverty line at 60% of that figure. In the United States, the poverty line is based on a Social Security system that makes certain arbitrary levels of income as poverty levels. The government then uses transfer payments to ensure a minimum income to all households based on a tangle of federal, state, and local regulations. While this is admirable from a social point of view, it remains vague and arbitrary from an economic perspective.

Absolute Poverty

Absolute levels of poverty exist only in economic theory. It is not economically possible to project a **universal poverty line** for all individuals in the world. This imaginary poverty line cannot fluctuate even if income distribution changes. The theoretical basis for this universal poverty line is that there is a minimum amount of goods necessary to survive and that that amount does not vary worldwide. To accurately compute such a figure, the total of all consumption must be known and accounted for. This is not possible from a practical point of view. **Absolute poverty** will decline when everyone's income in an economy rises, even if the distribution of wealth does not change. An absolute poverty rate may decline, regardless of whether inequality is remedied, as long as the neediest obtain some increase in income. From this brief analysis, it can be seen that an absolute poverty line is meaningless in and of itself. Unless a comparison of income levels within the same economy is measured, there is never a guarantee of accurate and meaningful poverty lines.

Relative Poverty

Only when a poverty line is fixed in relationship to other economic information does it have validity in the real world. A poverty line must be **relative** to some other economic indicator. For example, median income may be a relative standard with which to measure poverty. One could then define poverty as a certain percentage of income below the median income. In such a case, the general increase in income in a society may increase, but the poverty line will remain the same. Poverty can be thought of as inequality in income, rather than a specific level of income. An evening of income distribution will cause relative poverty to fall. Welfare economists sometimes prefer the term *inequality* to *relative poverty*. The subjective nature of defining poverty is apparent. For example, a level of income that more than takes care of necessities may still be relatively low for the economy as a whole. The arbitrary assignment of a poverty level relative to other economic measurements is by definition subjective.

Social Costs

Every economic decision has a **social cost** closely linked to it. The technical definition of the social costs of an economic action is the aggregate cost of that activity to society as a whole, as well as any costs incurred by the unit or agency making the decision. **Negative externality** is a situation that takes place when the social cost to society is greater than the cost to the decision-maker. The classic example of negative externality is manufacturing pollution. This has a huge social (and economic) cost that is seldom paid for directly by the firm causing the pollution. When the costs are greater to the private sector than to society, a **positive externality** is in effect. Social costs are a major topic and economic measurement in welfare economics. Activists measure social costs and employ them in their arguments for social, political, and economic policy.

Purposes and Effects of Taxation

Any assessment or charge to an individual economic unit by a government or quasi-government may be termed a **tax**. Some taxes are **direct**, such as a sales tax on goods and services sold. Other taxes may be **indirect**, property taxes being a prime example. Taxation has a long history dating back to biblical times. It is often mentioned in the Old and New Testaments. Earlier economic systems received "taxes" as goods and services rendered to a ruling authority. In contemporary economics, we usually think of taxes in terms of legal currency. Taxes have caused revolutions ("No taxation without representation"), have overturned governments, and have become a social and political issue of controversy and debate. Who should pay taxes, how much should be paid, and the use of tax revenue are all critical issues in the fabric of society. The branch of formal economics most concerned with taxes is public finance.

Taxation

Nations, states, and local governments use taxes to finance their operations and for special purposes. **Tax revenues** are typically used for public utilities, promoting of public safety and defense, reinvesting in capital improvement and replacement projects for the public, general operating expenses of the state, and funding public and welfare services. Other uses for tax revenues include social benefits for retired and disabled citizens, public transportation systems, compensation for those unable to work, educational uses, public health and healthcare systems, and waste removal operations. Governments also use taxes to stimulate or contract the economy, alter resource allocations in the economic system, ensure an equitable tax burden on all citizens, and change patterns of income distribution for members of society. Taxation and its revenues have become an important proactive tool for economists attempting to fine-tune macroeconomic activities.

Tax Rates

Tax rates are a percentage figure levied on the tax base to raise revenues. When the tax base is a good, service, or property, the tax is called an **ad valorem tax**. Examples of ad valorem taxes are common, including most property and sales taxes. Value-added taxes, common in Western Europe, add a "hidden" tax to all goods and services (with a few exceptions), computed on the added value at each stage of the manufacturing process. An **excise tax** is a tax levied on a tax base of a determined figure. Excess profit taxes are an example of an excise tax. Tax rates may be either marginal rates or average rates. To compute the **average tax rate**, the total tax revenue is compared to the total tax base as a ratio. **Marginal tax rates** are those imposed on the next unit of currency earned. For example, in a progressive income taxation system, the marginal tax rate will differ from person to person, depending on their income. **Tax brackets** are typically the framework for determining marginal rates of taxes at various income levels.

Flat, Progressive, and Regressive Taxation

A flat tax is one in which the same tax rate applies to all levels of income. For example, a country may have an income tax of 40% on every taxpayer's income, regardless of the level. Someone earning $10,000 a year would pay 40% of that figure. Another individual earning $100,000 a year would pay the same tax rate, 40%, but the dollar amount would differ dramatically. **Regressive tax systems** have a reduced schedule of tax rates as income rises. Thus, someone making $10,000 a year would pay a higher tax rate than someone making $100,000 a year. **Progressive income tax systems**, on the other hand, tax higher levels of income more than lower levels. Progressive tax systems are thought to be the most fair, as they place the largest tax burden on those with the most income. People are seldom happy with any system of taxation, and the entire issue has become a political one, with almost all people calling for tax reform of one type or another.

Income Tax

Most income tax systems in modern economies are **progressive** in that they increase the tax rate as income rises. Progressive tax systems are favored by those who feel the brunt of taxation should be on those who can more easily afford it. Conservative economists (and politicians) argue that this form of taxation is punishing the economically successful and is a deterrent to economic growth. The nature of tax collection and the private information required to administer the system angers some who feel the government is increasingly intrusive in their lives. The nature of tax collection was revolutionized by the concept of **withholding** taxes directly from an individual's paycheck. This serves to aid tax compliance, as the taxes are automatically collected each pay period. Psychologically, it seems less burdensome to the taxpayer who never actually has the money. People have come to accept their salaries as being "take home pay," the actual disposable income available to them after taxes are withheld.

Capital Gains and Corporation Taxes

Capital gains taxes may be levied whenever a major capital asset is sold. **Capital gains taxes** may be applied as a regular tax when the capital gain is called income. In certain circumstances, special tax rates apply to capital gains, and a part of the gain is exempt from taxation. **Corporations** and affluent individuals are the beneficiaries of capital gains tax schedules. Tax rules, statutes, and tax codes provide a number of tax shelters for corporations. Tax "loopholes" are exploited by corporate tax attorneys and accountants to minimize the tax burden of corporations. Income earned by corporations also may benefit from special tax rates. Depreciation of major assets and deductions for major assets provide favorable tax breaks for corporations. Corporations may exempt or defer taxes from income flow by using these special considerations. **Corporate taxes** are often the targets of criticism from social and economic activists who feel they are granted special privileges not available to individuals.

Property Taxes, Inheritance Tax, and Personal Property Tax

Real estate is subject to taxation in the form of a **property tax**. Property taxes may also be levied by governments for personal property such as automobiles. The usual method of determining a property tax is to assess the value of the property on a regular basis and apply the existing tax rate to this base. Property taxes are a prime method of financing education in the United States. Taxes on **estates** and on **inheritances** have both their advocates and critics. Some believe large estates should be taxed, as they are most able to pay. Others argue this discriminates against the wealthy and economically successful individuals. As mentioned above, **personal property taxes** may be levied on many kinds of assets, including vehicles and boats. Critics argue there is no rationale for these taxes and they simply serve to fill government coffers. Auto registration and license fees at least offer a privilege (driving) for their levy.

International Trade and Tariffs

Tariffs are, in effect, a tax on goods imported from other countries. Goods cannot be delivered and sold before a tariff is paid. **Tariffs** have broad implications in international trade and, consequently, in relations between nations. Tariffs may be calculated by the weight of goods, or as a percentage of the value of the item (ad valorem). Sometimes, governments impose tariffs as a purely money-making function, and these are termed **revenue tariffs**. Tariffs are widely used by countries to protect their own exports and to defend their own industries from competition from abroad. Tariffs add to the price of imported goods, affording a price advantage to local products. A protective tariff can be so high as to be prohibitive, so that no imports are economically viable. Tariffs have become both political and economic weapons for competing nations. Tariffs have historically been opposed by "free traders," who believe unfettered trade is the healthiest economic environment and works to the benefit of all countries involved.

Evolutionary Economics in Depth

Evolutionary economics is a new and growing field in heteroeconomics. Modeled on the life sciences, it looks at economic activity as complex, dynamic interactions with elements of scarcity, growth, and the striving for competitive advantages. In a sense, **evolutionary economics** imposes Darwin's theory of evolution on economic conditions to explain both behavior and results. **Survival of the fittest** may be applied to business concerns, with the most adaptable succeeding and those unable to select economic survival capabilities failing and forced to suspend operations. Firms must survive by combining a product mix appropriate for their markets with effective business practices. As conditions change, those businesses that are able to maintain flexibility and measured responses to a changing economic environment will survive, while less responsive firms will fall away. Companies that succeed tend to continue innovative practices that allow them to achieve success. Those who fail to respond to economic change will not survive in the long run.

Agricultural Economics

Agricultural economics reflects a more businesslike approach to economics and is focused on the individual units active in agricultural activities. Courses in **agricultural economics** in colleges and universities tend to emphasize business practices as they relate to agriculture. By definition, this gives agricultural economics a microeconomic flavor. The field of study in agricultural economics relates to the supply of farm commodities and domestic animals. Included in the broader scope of the field are the area of rural development, the economics of production for farm goods, and the business-oriented areas of agribusiness management. Although a specialized field of economics, general economic principles such as risk, resource allocation, markets, competition, and international trade are all an important part of agricultural economics. Specialized topics include food safety, crop protection, farm production methods and techniques, rules and regulations governing agricultural economics, and the critical importance of the field to the well-being of society.

Direct and Indirect Taxation

Direct taxes are defined as those that are imposed and collected directly from the economic units being taxed. For example, income taxes are levied and collected from the individual or business that actually receives monies as income. **Indirect taxes**, by contrast, are collected from a third party who is not the being actually taxed. Value-added taxes are indirect taxes, hidden from the consumer who pays an increased retail or wholesale price that includes the value-added tax. **Statutes** determine for whom the tax is being collected. The individual who ends up paying the tax is another matter. For example, a tax may be placed on alcoholic beverages of all kinds. Only those who choose to consume these products will actually be subject to the tax. Laws of supply and demand in the marketplace will determine the individuals that will pay this tax. If an individual chooses not to buy wine, beer, or liquor, they will be, in effect, exempt from that tax. The more a person consumes the taxed items, the more tax will be paid by that individual.

Chapter Quiz

Ready to see how well you retained what you just read? Scan the QR code to go directly to the chapter quiz interface for this study guide. If you're using a computer, simply visit the online resources page at **mometrix.com/resources719/aepaeconomics** and click the Chapter Quizzes link.

Macroeconomics, Economic Theories, and International Economics

Microeconomics and Macroeconomics

While microeconomics studies the individual units of economic activity, **macroeconomics** takes a larger view. It is the analysis of the **aggregate** of all the economic actions of individuals, corporations, and businesses. This expanded scope includes the issues of government policies to influence the economy. Such national goals include suppressing inflation, stimulating the economy through monetary and fiscal policies, and attaining a maximum employment level. The conduct and regulation of international trade is another area of national interest. There are multiple economic schools of thought that influence macroeconomics. Macroeconomics is an area of continuing evolution, and various tools of economic analysis are used from a variety of sources. The goal of all such schools is to provide the most current and precise economic data and analysis available. Pieces of research carried out by different patterns of economic thinking are combined to produce the most useful and accurate information.

Review Video: Microeconomics and Macroeconomics
Visit mometrix.com/academy and enter code: 538837

Analytical Approaches in Macroeconomics

The two broad divisions of economic analysis are **Keynesian theory**, developed in the 20th century by the English economist John Maynard Keynes, and **supply-side economics**, a current favorite of more conservative economists. Keynesian economics proposes government action to stimulate demand in an economy. Supply-side economics is concerned with the policies that will encourage increased supply by manufacturers and other business organizations. Keynes believed that aggregate demand was the key to understanding fluctuations in the economy. He argued for strong government interventions to attain these goals. Much of the New Deal economics applied during the depression of the 1930s was based on Keynes' theories. The so-called "supply-siders" emphasize the role of the aggregate money supply and fiscal action (or inaction) as the crucial factors in economic growth.

Modern Schools of Macroeconomics

Milton Friedman, a University of Chicago economist, was the chief proponent of **monetarism**, which states that the supply of money in an economy is the major determinant of economic growth or deflation. It eschews the manipulation of aggregate demand in favor of monetary policy that controls the amount of money available in an economy. **Keynesian economics** encourages the proactive role of the government in stimulating aggregate demand to promote economic growth. An offshoot of this school is **New Keynesian economics**, which combines traditional Keynesian theory with microeconomic tools in order to spur demand.

The **Post-Keynesian theorists** incorporate much of Keynesian economics but believe historical patterns in economics lead to more uncertainty in applying economic stimuli to promote demand. **New classical economics** adds the concept of rational expectations to the Keynesian mix. **Austrian economics** is a conservative school that believes the government's activity in economic policy leads to fluctuations in the business cycles.

Milton Friedman

The strongest advocate of the monetary school of macroeconomics was Milton Friedman, an American economist whose theories have become associated with minimal government intervention except in the regulation of the money supply. A Nobel Prize winner in 1976, Friedman's work has included the analysis of **consumption**, as well as an emphasis on **monetary theory and policy**. Friedman has become an icon of conservative economists and politicians for his stance against government spending to spur the economy. Friedman believed that inflation is a direct result of an increase in the money supply and that monetary policy is the most effective tool in managing an economic system. His rejection of government's proactive role in increasing aggregate demand is controversial because it goes against the major themes of government activity of the last 70 years. He argued against many of the Keynesian interventions that have become part of contemporary economics.

Scope of Political Economy

The economic activity and policy of the state are major concerns of **political economy**. Questions such as the level of unemployment, budget surpluses or deficits, and general economic well-being are all important concepts in political economy. Political economy may be said to include all methods of production and distribution of excess funds or remedy of deficits in an economy. The importance of structural relationships in a society is the basis of political economy. The field of general economics places more importance on the allocation of scarce resources to satisfy unlimited demand. Political economy, because it includes social and political elements, is a broader field in a sense. The historical role of a country is very important in political economy. For example, the history of serfdom in Russia set the stage for communism in the early part of the 20th century. American self-reliance and independence set a framework for capitalism to prosper. These historical precedents must be included in the study of political economy.

Balance of Payments

The net sum of a country's exports and imports is known as the **balance of payments** for a country. These trade activities include finished products, raw materials, financial resources, and transfer payments. If the sum total of cash and liquid assets flowing into a country is greater than the outflow, the country has a **positive balance of payments**. If the opposite is the case, the country has a **negative balance of payments. International accounts** include current accounts derived from the net flow of assets resulting from the trade of goods, services, and transfer payments. The accounting of funds received from sales and purchases of financial instruments is called a country's **capital account**. The **foreign reserves account** includes international funds, gold, and balances in exchange accounts. The sum of all these accounts determines the balance of payments for a country.

Monetary System

As in other markets, the same elements of analysis may be used for the **money market**. The laws of demand and supply apply to the money market and result in market equilibrium for the price of money. The quantity of money in the system is also a product of these forces. Money in circulation includes actual paper money and coins. Paper money may be banknotes or Federal Reserve notes that are physically produced by the United State's mint but represent money created by the Federal Reserve based on the credit of the federal government. This credit is electronically created by the government to influence the economy. In reality, since all paper money is based on the promise of the government to honor the currency, all notes are electronically produced. Coins may be produced outside of the Federal Reserve system by legislation. The total money supply is within the scope of the **Federal Reserve System**.

The **money supply** may be measured in a number of ways. Technically, money may be defined as anything that is used to pay a debt, but in practice, money is defined as the currency and coins in circulation. Economic analysis of money uses symbols to designate different measurements of money. The widest definition of money is as "a store of value." In the United States, the Federal Reserve designates the definitions of money measured by various computations. The total of all coins and notes in circulation at any given time is designated by the notation **M0**. **M1:M0** represents all funds in circulation plus all checking and savings accounts (demand deposits). **M2** adds to this money market funds and certificates of deposit held by all investors. These definitions are helpful in monetary analysis by designating components of the money supply in various measurements.

Monetary Exchange Equation and the Current Money Supply

One of the most widely used monetary analytical tools is the **money exchange equation** which provides a link between the money supply and inflation or deflation. Elements of the money exchange equation are the **velocity of money**, defined as the number of times money turns over; the **Gross Domestic Product** (value of all goods and services produced in a period); and the **Gross Domestic Product Deflator**, a measure of inflation in the economy. For instance, M1 in the United States in 2010 was over $1.8 trillion and then over $6.7 trillion in 2020. The M2 figure for the country was over $8.8 trillion in 2010 and then over $19.3 trillion by the end of 2020.

Creation of Money

The total money supply can only be increased (with the exception of coinage) by banks creating new funds through the Federal Reserve System's **electronic crediting process**, where notes are exchanged for electronic credits. The broader definitions of the money supply include demand deposits or checking and savings accounts, plus certificates of deposit. Banks list **demand deposits** as their major assets. A fraction of these deposits may be loaned, thus creating "new" money. That process may be repeated a number of times to expand the money supply. The Federal Reserve controls the amount of new money that can be created by setting a minimum reserve requirement for banks to hold against their total demand deposits. Raising the reserve requirement limits the amount of new money that can be created, while lowering the reserve requirement allows for an expansion of the money supply.

Function of Bank Reserves at the Central Bank

To create additional funds in the money supply, the **central bank** (The Federal Reserve in the United States) may buy a quantity of government securities on the open market, thus increasing money available for banks to lend out under the fractional reserve system. This will increase the total money supply. To reduce the money supply, the central bank sells government securities on the open market and depletes the funds in the private banks. In this manner, the Federal Reserve maintains some control over the total money in circulation. **Private banks**, in turn, loan out a percentage of the funds, which, in effect, creates new money. The funds may then be turned over or multiplied many times, increasing the impact of the initial increase in money.

Money Market Instruments

There are a variety of money market securities or instruments available for trading. A common type is a draft or bill drawn on a bank, which guarantees full payment of the amount. This is known as a "**banker's acceptance**." Promissory notes or drafts have a specific maturity date and are sold at a discount on the open market. Time deposits with specific maturity dates and a specified rate of interest are known as **certificates of deposit**. Short-term government securities such as **Treasury Bills** are issued by various federal or quasi-federal agencies. Federal securities include deposits held by the Federal Reserve at any of their branches or agencies. These notes all carry an interest charge. Cities, towns, and counties often float short-term issues to finance specific projects or general operations. Treasury Bills are very short-term securities issued by the Federal government and are traded on the open market.

CURRENCY

Currency may be defined technically as any legal tender with which debts may be settled. **Currency's** major use is to facilitate the exchange of goods and services in the marketplace. The world is divided into "currency zones" that determine what currency may be used in trade. Rates of exchange are a market where different currencies may be bought and sold. Both banknotes and coins are considered currency. The country that issues the currency owns a **monopoly** in that market. Central banks of countries are the institutions that control currency (and the money supply) through monetary and fiscal policy. These central banks or other monetary authorities (set up as an agency by the government) control and implement monetary policy and activity. Such authorities differ in their power from country to country. For example, in the United States, the Federal Reserve is a wholly independent agency free of political controls. Although Congress legislated the Federal Reserve into existence, it remains completely independent in its activity.

GOLD STANDARD

A monetary system linked to the value of gold is said to be on the **gold standard**. Those who issue currency agree to exchange banknotes and coins for gold based on a fixed exchange rate. Thus, gold becomes the basic unit of account to measure all wealth against. Gold standards were created to stabilize currencies by making it impossible for governments to create money at their pleasure. The gold standard also protects against hyperinflation and the overexpansion of debt in an economy. Originally, when the major form of money was coins (usually silver or gold) there was a logic to the gold standard. The gold standard was once a common phenomenon among nations but has now been replaced by systems giving the central banks of countries the power to create money and manipulate monetary policy for the good of the economy. No modern country would return to the gold standard despite the protection it affords.

HISTORICAL USE OF GOLD AS STORE OF VALUE

Gold was historically considered to be the ideal measure of wealth and a practical unit of account for market transactions. **Gold** was rare, easily measured and divided (originally by weight), extremely durable, and provided a uniform measure of value that transcended geographical boundaries, making it ideal for settling debts between nations or individuals living in different areas. Gold may be easily transported and was used as a convenient base for the early banking systems in the world. Banknotes and other forms of paper currencies have obvious practical advantages over gold. Besides providing central banks with the power to create money, paper currencies are portable and resistant to hoarding,. The complexity of the world economy made gold obsolete in the modern world except as an investment or reserve. International trade in the modern world could not be conducted with gold as the measure of value.

THEORY OF THE GOLD STANDARD

The **central rationale** for the gold standard is the theory that an increase in the money supply will cause inflation. If there is speculation over the value of money in the future, **uncertainty** will erode economic growth. Such uncertainty about the true value of money leads to a chaotic economy. The gold standard was implemented in most cases to stem this uncertainty. The gold standard would guarantee confidence in the economy, and benefit both domestic and international commerce. A second reason for instituting the gold standard was to put stringent limits on the role of the central bank in controlling the economy. Governments were thought to be inept in economic affairs, and the gold standard ensured a limit on their participation. The gold standard would also build confidence in money markets and inspire individuals and businesses to boost economic activity without fear of government intervention.

GOLD AS A RESERVE TODAY

Today, gold is held by nations to protect their currencies and provide a stable reserve of stored value in an economy. Gold tends to **fluctuate** with the rise and fall of the dollar on exchange markets. When the dollar depreciates in relation to other currencies, the value of gold rises. Thus, gold serves as a stable financial asset in the portfolios of almost all central banks in the world. It serves a type of **internal reserve** that may be called upon should adverse economic conditions arise. Banks may also use gold as a reserve against loans to their own governments as well as international trading partners. Banks seek to hold in reserve assets with "real value" rather than electronically produced money. They may add real property, silver, and other stable assets to protect themselves. International banks also tend to hold significant amounts of United States dollars because of the stability inherent in the American economy. Central banks must feel they have stable assets to meet any economic crisis that might arise.

INFLATION

Inflation strikes when there is a general price increase of goods and services against one currency. A price index, such as the **Consumer Price Index**, can be used as a measuring tool to compare prices at different times. A fictional "market basket" of commonly consumed staples is measured and charted over a period of time (usually one year). If the price of the representative market basket has gone up, **inflation** has occurred. For example, if a typical basket costs $500 this year as compared to $400 last year for the same basket, inflation has risen over a year. Inflation reduces the buying power of money, and if uncontrolled, can threaten the entire economy. An example of **runaway inflation** occurred in Germany in the 1930s. Inflation was rampant and people had to take large quantities of physical money to markets to exchange for goods and services. This rampant inflation helped bring the Nazis to power. **Deflation**, the general lowering of prices and the subsequent increase in purchasing power of money is a much less frequent phenomena.

MEASUREMENT

Measuring inflation can be an inexact science, because there are a number of price indexes that can be utilized. Most price indexes are based on information gleaned through government agencies and institutions. To accurately **measure the rate of inflation**, hypothetical market baskets of goods are compared from year to year. An adjustment termed a **hedonic adjustment** may be applied if there is a change in the makeup of the basket of goods. The weight given to each product or service in the basket will affect the rate of inflation. The **inflation rate** is the percentage rate of the price increase from one year to the next on identical bundles of goods. The United States has suffered through some significant periods of inflation, particularly after World War II. Europe has been plagued with hyperinflation, which is an extreme rise in prices due to the fall of the purchasing power of money. Such hyperinflation destabilizes economies and may result in political and social crises, as well as an economic one.

Indexes: There are a number of indexes that may be used to chart the rise of inflation. Perhaps the most common one is the **cost-of-living index**, which seeks to measure how much it actually costs an individual to live for a specified period of time. This index is measured by the **Consumer Price Index**, which prices bundles of goods and services and compares them over time. Another reliable measuring tool is the **Producer Price Index**, which accounts for the actual amount of money the producer of goods and services receives. This is a net figure that considers other economic realities such as taxes in the computation. **Commodity price indexes** focus on changes in prices of essential commodities used in an economy. They are widely used in agricultural economics. There are indexes that measure price changes in products sold by wholesalers, which are then passed on to retailers for sale to consumers. Some indexes attempt to pinpoint the personal consumption of individuals, but this is difficult to do with any degree of accuracy.

Misery Index

The "Misery Index" was developed to measure the economic hardships of combined unemployment and inflation. Although controversial, this index attempts to ascertain the level of economic impact on citizens in a society beset with the twin problems of **inflation** and **unemployment**. Economists have not been able to agree on the effect of such an index on individuals or businesses. There is a school of thought that argues that previous histories of inflation linked to economic unhappiness have conditioned the public to regard any increase in inflation to be cause for concern. For example, a relatively low level of rising prices may have a psychological impact beyond the economic one. Some inflation is considered necessary to balance the business cycle during periods of recession. One could say that the public takes a much dimmer view of inflation than do economists. This difference becomes important if the public reacts negatively to minor inflation and it becomes an expectation of a weakened economy.

Causes

Pinpointing the **causes** of inflation is an area of controversy. Monetary theory holds that inflation is a direct result of an increase in the money supply without a corresponding growth of the entire economy. In the most simple terms, this means the amount of money available for consumption will be the prime determinant of spending in the economy. Neo-Keynesian economists feel that the injection into the economy of large expenditures by the government and its agencies is a goad to economic growth. They posit the theory of **demand-pull inflation**, where the demand by consumers for goods and services and the inability of the economy to respond to increased demand cause prices to rise. **Cost-push inflation** is the result of a sudden and unexpected increase in the cost of an essential product or service. Some believe that inflation is a permanent feature of a modern economy, where guaranteed wage increases and adaptive economic behavior based on past history ensure some level of inflation will occur regularly in an economy.

Strategies for Combating Inflation

Most modern countries are in a constant struggle with **inflation**. There are several strategies employed to keep price increases at an acceptable level. Central banks have the power to fight inflation by applying monetary policy and, most importantly, by setting interest rates. When inflation threatens an economy, the raising of interest rates acts as a deterrent to price increases by making money more costly and slowing the economic activity of a country. Central banks have the autonomy to apply these measures when they feel they are appropriate. An imposition of wage and price controls is a more drastic way to slow or halt inflation. These measures have many drawbacks, including the possibility of depressing the economy too far. Controls also promote hoarding and artificial shortages and sometimes encourage the creation of alternative marketplaces that impair economic growth.

Hyperinflation

Runaway, or hyperinflation, is an economic crisis in which prices rise at an alarming rate as currency becomes devalued. There are no accurate measurements for **hyperinflation**, but economists agree a general and rapid raising of prices without a corresponding movement toward equilibrium is a recipe for runaway inflation. True hyperinflation is recognized when governments are forced to dramatically increase the money supply as currency loses value. Most hyperinflation is created by the printing of vast quantities of **paper money** to attempt to react to price increases. This usually initiates a spiral of increasing prices and decreasing value of the currency. This cycle is difficult to break, because expectations of individuals and businesses are for yet more rising prices and devalued money. A common reaction to hyperinflation is the use of hard money as a store of value and medium of exchange.

Stagflation

When high inflation is joined by a depressed economy and high unemployment, the result has been called "**stagflation**." Unexpected changes to an aggregate supply can create an economic trauma that has implications for the entire economy. Stagflation creates a dilemma for central banks. If the bank chooses to stimulate the economy by lowering the reserve requirements for commercial banks and reducing the interest rates, it runs the risk of generating too much money, which will increase inflation. Should the bank elect to combat inflation by raising the interest rates and the reserve requirement of banks, these actions could depress the economy further and result in more unemployment. Both choices have significant negative results for a struggling economy. When the United States faced this dilemma in the 1970s, it was thought to have been caused by the failure of the government to gauge prices. The ultimate response to this period of stagflation was the emergence of supply-side economics as a strategic tool. Economists disagree on the effectiveness of this strategy.

Qualities of Money

All money or forms of exchange share common characteristics which define the store of value of the currency used. Money must be a generally accepted medium for trading and settling debts. Acceptance of money depends on trust in the **issuing institution or nation**.

To be useful as a deferred payment instrument, money must serve as a basic unit of account in an economic system. This requisite is fulfilled if money is seen to be a **standard of value** through which other goods may be given comparative value. The relative cost of any good or service must be measured against a standard which is the value of money. Perhaps most importantly, money must be accepted as a **store of value** by everyone in an economy. In this manner, money is a representation of the essential worth of any traded good or service. The system of deferred payment under which most markets operate makes it imperative that money has its own essential store of value resting on the promise of a central bank or nation to honor the currency.

Effects of Money in Economics

Money is an essential element in economics and forms the basis for individual, business, and government markets. Both the quality and the quantity of money affect the economy in fundamental ways. Central banks manipulate **money quantities** in order to influence the economy by expanding or contracting available funds. **Monetary policies** of nations have an important impact on the economies of those countries. It can be used to stimulate growth or to slow an overheated economy. **Monetary failure** in a economy produces uncertainty and chaotic markets. When the USSR dissolved in the early 1990s, a financial crisis occurred that still impacts some nations. Defining money in the modern world can be difficult due to the myriad of forms of credit available globally. The revolution started by credit cards in the last 50 years has completely changed the nature of exchange in most markets. Money has many substitutes, including demand deposits, savings accounts, and credit and debit cards, which serve as a store of value that is generally accepted.

Shrinking the Money Supply

Sometimes, monetary policy demands a **reduction** in the quantity of money available in the economy. Central banks have the power to destroy or remove from circulation coins and paper currency at their discretion. Only a small fraction of the total money supply is represented by coins and notes. Money is **destroyed** when government securities are purchased and when debt is paid off or canceled. Buying government bonds or other federal or state notes and paper takes that money out of the system. If a debt is paid to an institution such as a commercial bank, that money is lost from the total supply of funds. The Treasury of the United States is empowered to reduce the money supply through open market operations or retiring government debt. When money is withdrawn from a bank, the money supply is reduced because the bank can no longer loan out the funds and thereby create new money.

Measures of National Income and Output

National income may be defined as the aggregate figure of all consumption, individual, business, and governmental income, plus total investments and the balance of trade accounts for a country. This aggregate number, derived from adding these categories together, is called the **expenditure method** of national income determination. Another calculation to determine the national income is to account for all the goods and services produced in a country during a fixed period. This is called the **production accounting** of national income. Yet another way of computing national income is to total all income received by individuals, businesses, and governments to arrive at total national income. This is the **income approach** to national income accounting. To summarize, there are three ways of calculating national income: total expenditures, total value of production, and the aggregate consumption figures for a country.

GNP

The **Gross National Product** (GNP) is one of the prime indicators of the economic health of a country. Typically, this is an aggregate figure which includes all goods and services **produced** in the economy for a specified period, usually one year. This computation uses "final" goods and services to reach the aggregate production. This means that raw materials produced and sold to manufacturers are not included if they are to be used to make final products that are then sold as final goods. GNP reflects only new final products for the measurement period are counted; markets and transactions in used goods are omitted from GNP. Allocations of GNP are decided by the nation that owns the business unit, not where the goods are sold. For example, funds received from a Volvo manufactured and sold in the United States would be counted as part of Sweden's GNP, as they are the owners of the corporation. This means that all proceeds of sales of final goods belong in the national account of the country that claims ownership of the firm that sold the goods.

GDP

Another important measure of economic health is **Gross Domestic Product** (GDP). This calculation aggregates all goods and services sold in a specified period but allocates monies determined by where the **sale** actually takes place, rather than what country owns the business. A Volvo automobile manufactured and sold in the United States would be included in the GDP of America because it was earned in the United States, even though the business owners are Swedish. It follows that to compute GNP from GDP, the aggregate total of income from goods sold by other countries must be subtracted from GDP. Gross Domestic Product is a strong indicator of the short-term health of an economy as it measures current aggregate production. It is not as reliable a measure for accounting for the sources, and allocations of a country's income. GDP is a better measure of the state of production in the short term. GNP is better when analyzing sources and uses of income.

Gross Value Added, Depreciation, and Net National Product

A significant portion of GNP is reserved and used for refurbishing and maintaining the productive capacity of a country. This includes monies used to repair and replace capital equipment that has become obsolete or inefficient. This total **depreciation** is the amount of GNP reserved for the replacement and service of capital goods. The **national income approach** is a calculation of the total income earned in a period, minus depreciation, indirect taxes, and direct taxes. **Personal income**, a major component of the income method, is the net national income minus taxes, retained earnings, and transfer payments by governments. **Personal disposable income**, the amount of income available for consumption is the total personal income minus personal taxes and plus transfer payments. It is useful for economists to break down categories in order to analyze the interactions and relationships between elements of income earned in a country.

National Income and Welfare

There are many ways to measure the **welfare** of an individual in an economy. Although non-economic issues affect welfare to a large degree, economic welfare can be measured mathematically. Dividing the total net disposable income by the total population gives an economic value to welfare. Using economic value as an indicator, there is a correlation between this figure and various other measures of welfare. Some problems exist in any attempt to measure actual **disposable income**. There is a significant amount of unpaid economic activity, including domestic functions such as the care of children. Mothers who are "employed" in childcare and running homes are not included in national income, which is an obvious flaw in the calculation. Other factors important to welfare are the quality of life, which includes social well-being; freedom from ecological pollution; and political and religious choice. These factors are only indirectly measured in the welfare of individuals in a society.

Real and Nominal Values

In the analysis of GNP, there are inherent problems. Due to the presence of inflation, price levels rise virtually every year, leading to a rise in "nominal" increase in GNP, even if there is no increase in production or income. This gives an unrealistic picture of GNP and paints an optimistic picture that is not entirely accurate. This figure is called **"nominal" GNP**. **Real GNP** is the nominal figure adjusted for inflation. If inflation is five percent, this figure must be applied to the total income or production figures to find real value. An accurate computation of GNP must compare gross figures of income or production for two periods by designating values of goods and services after inflation. This real GNP is a much more accurate measurement of the growth and health of an economy. The higher the rate of inflation the larger the differential between nominal and real national income.

Wealth

The definition of wealth is both an objective and subjective one. In common usage, **wealth** is understood to consist primarily of money, land, and investments of an individual. However, wealth includes many subjective factors that cannot be measured by strictly economic values. Additionally, concepts of wealth differ between cultures and societies. **Economic wealth** must be measured in relation to all other individuals in the same economic systems. The income of a middle-class American would make a third-world citizen very wealthy. Within the United States, cost-of-living, income, and taxes vary widely. A wealthy person in Iowa may not be considered wealthy in Los Angeles because of differences in the economic situations of the two places. Additionally, intangibles such as environmental health, health of the individual, quality of life, and dozens of other less objective factors all must be accounted for in considering **real wealth**.

Monetary Policy

The managing of the economy by manipulating and adjusting the money supply is called **monetary policy**. Usually addressing specific goals, monetary policy includes adjusting prime interest rates, buying or selling government securities in open market operations, and setting reserve requirements for commercial banks. The higher the reserve requirement, the less funds are available for expansion of the money supply. Two major elements are in play in monetary policy: the **amount** of money in the economy and the level of **interest rates** (the cost of using money).

Monetary policy is geared to affect each of these variables in order to influence the economy. Monetary policy may be easy, with lower interest rates and reserve requirements, or tighter, with higher interest rates and higher reserve requirements. Monetary policy as an economic policy is favored by more conservative economists and politicians, while more liberal analysts prefer Keynesian methods stimulating aggregate demand.

History

The use of **monetary policy** as a major factor in influencing the economy is a fairly recent phenomenon, beginning in the 18th century and becoming a common strategy since the 1950s. Originally, monetary policy concerned itself with increasing or decreasing the supply of money in the economy. Now, much more sophisticated methods involving a bevy of financial tools and types of interventions. Monetary policy in its broadest sense includes both long- and short-term interest rates, the quality and quantity of credit available, and the purchase and sale of government securities. It seeks to deter government action to influence aggregate demand through injections of money into the economy. Monetary policy also influences exchange rates, the velocity of money in the economy, and the ownership of securities in the economy. The most extreme position on monetary policy is a return to the gold standard. This is a minority position held by only a few fringe economists. To adopt the gold standard would severely limit other tools of monetary policy.

Trends in Central Banking

As monetary policy has become more proactive in modern economies, more sophisticated tools have been employed to **influence the economy**. The monetary level could be changed only by relatively crude methods, particularly when the gold standard was in place. Now, central banks are active in the sale and purchase of **government long- and short-term securities**, which provides a tool for expansion or contraction of the money supply. Selling government securities takes money out of the supply, while buying these instruments injects new money into the system. The other method used effectively by monetary policy is **changing the reserve requirements** for commercial banks. An increase in the reserve requirement contracts the supply of money by compelling banks to keep a higher percentage of demand deposits. A reduction of the reserve requirement allows commercial banks to lend out more funds, increasing the money supply. Interest rates may also be lowered on secured loans to banks. If the rate is lowered enough, commercial banks will borrow from the central bank and loan out these funds in turn.

Inflation Targeting

Monetary policy may be used as a tool to limit **inflation**. This goal is attained by **raising the rate of interest**, which tends to restrain economic growth and tighten money. The Federal Reserve chairman announces periodic reviews and incremental adjustments to the interest rates as deemed necessary for the health of the economy. When the rate of interest is raised, it will cost commercial banks more to borrow from the central bank, thus cooling the economy. Although the interest rates are determined by an independent agency, they are subject to both social and political influence. In the United States, a committee of the Federal Reserve Bank monitors and adjusts interest rates. Close attention is given to the economic information that indicates inflation is rising, falling, or steady. A defined goal of the central bank is to control inflation; therefore, monitoring indicators in the economy is an ongoing task. The chairman of the Federal Reserve has become a familiar public figure due to multiple appearances before Congress to give reports on the state of the economy.

Federal Reserve and Creation of Money

An example of how money is **created** may be understood by following the flow of funds. Suppose someone deposits $100 in his or her commercial bank. Assuming a reserve requirement of 10%, the commercial bank creates more money by lending $90 to a qualified borrower. This increases the money supply by $190. The additional money may be used for consumption, savings, or investment. A second example would be the purchase of government securities. If commercial paper is purchased from an individual for $100, that individual has an extra $100 to consume, save, or invest. In any case, the amount of money in circulation has increased by $100. When the Federal Reserve lowers interest rates, both businesses and individuals are encouraged to borrow and consume. This tool has far-reaching effects in managing the economy.

Criticisms of Monetary Policy

Some schools of economics that favor markets free of government "interference" object to any monetary policy as a distortion of the marketplace. The so-called **Austrian school of economics** vehemently opposes monetary policy in any form. Advocates of market freedom argue that the "invisible hand" of self-interest should determine economic activity. In a situation of a free market, consumers will decide, based on their perceived self-interest, whether to consume goods now or at a later time. This is referred to as a saver's "**time presence**." Consumption now would deplete savings and cause a rise in interest rates due to the increased demand for money. Deferring consumption lowers the interest rate by reducing the demand for money. Critics of monetary policy say that such policies do not accurately reflect consumers' preferences, as they are artificially manipulated. When consumer preferences are ignored, businesses will often mistake lowered rates with consumer confidence and make poor investment choices.

National Income and Product Accounts

The accounting for national income uses traditional accounting procedures to report the state of the economy measured by aggregate income. Both businesses and government resources are used to prepare the reports. Typically, double-entry bookkeeping practices are used in recording the economic information. The left side of the report lists all earned income for the period, with salaries and wages being the most dominant numbers in the account. The right side of the report summarizes production information, including consumption, investment, savings, transfer payments, and net exports (balance of trade). Totals for the two sides must be the same when all economic factors are considered. **National income** represents the total income of employees, government income, rental income, corporate income, and the net balance of transfer payments. Each of these categories is subject to specific defining qualities to ensure the accounts are accurate.

Economic Growth

Although there are many ways to measure **economic growth**, the increase of the store of value is a common rule used in macroeconomic analysis. It may be understood as the aggregate wealth of an economic entity. A common calculation used to determine economic growth is to measure the aggregate value of all goods and services that an economy produces. A true measurement of economic growth must discount inflation to be an accurate evaluation. This is called **real-time measurement**. In formal economic analysis, economic growth is determined by the total production of an economy adjusted for price rises. Economists often use GDP to evaluate growth. Per capita GDP may indicate the level of the well-being of an individual in an economy. Per capita GDP does not account for all the factors that determine the well-being of people in an economy.

"Limits to Growth" Debate

Economic growth carries with it substantial costs, both measurable and intangible. Given a world of limited resources, economic growth includes the more rapid **depletion** of such resources. The combined effects of economic growth on air and water pollution are too great to be measured. The destruction of rainforests and extinction of plant and animal species at an unprecedented rate are added, and sometimes hidden, costs of economic growth. The combination of rapid growth and resource depletion may eventually **stop economic growth** completely. The introduction of new technology has fueled the rate of economic growth in the world. This technology may also be able to allow growth without many of the negative results. Many social scientists and economists contend growth must slow or stop in order to maintain a level of well-being that is acceptable. Others put faith in the ability of mankind to innovate and adjust to allow growth without devastating consequences.

Good and Bad Economic Growth

Often, economists involved in analysis and policy decisions work on the assumption that all growth is good, without regard to the social costs. From a strict economic perspective, almost all economic growth may be rationalized as worthwhile. Using these precepts, plans and policies that are damaging to the general welfare may be defended effectively. For example, opening natural habitats for exploration of fossil fuels seems to make economic sense given the demand for oil. The costs of such decisions is not always readily apparent, but over time degrades the quality of life. **Positive economic growth** involves the consideration of social and environmental factors in making economic policy. A successful economy does little good if the quality of life declines as a result of the growth. Economies exist for and because of the people and social systems they serve. If they fail to improve the general welfare, they have failed regardless of economic growth.

Purchasing Power Parity

In international trade or speculation in currency markets, there must be a tool that uses a common measurement to compare value. This tool is called **purchasing power parity**, which provides an estimate of the number of goods and services that can be purchased with different currencies. This tool is handy for understanding comparative value and measuring living standards in different countries. Differences in income levels in countries and fluctuations in price levels make purchasing power parity an important analytical tool when comparing the value of currencies. In international trade, it is imperative to know the equivalent value of the two countries trading so that each buyer and seller understands the purchasing power of the monies involved. Differences in prices, standard of living, production, and consumption variables are considered in the purchasing power parity calculation. This avoids complex analyses of independent variables in each country.

Rational Expectations

In macroeconomics, the concept of **rational expectations** is used to provide a model of the results of economic decisions. The theory of rational expectations was first posited in the early 1960s as a refined tool for understanding the results of proposed economic actions. This theory has proved exceptionally useful in evaluating macroeconomic trends in **Keynesian economic theory**. For example, a business may wish to make a pricing change in a product and needs to know how this would affect sales and income. The rational expectations model would project the impact of the price change on the business. In a sense, rational expectations are an informed guess after considering all available economic information. The theory cannot make predictions about human behavior in the marketplace without assumptions to provide a frame of reference. Outcomes that are forecast using this model do not differ significantly from the state of market equilibrium. Rational expectation models form the foundations of **efficient markets theory**.

Unemployment

In economics, an **unemployed** person is one who has the will and capacity to work, but cannot find meaningful employment. The total number of unemployed people as a ratio to the entire labor pool is the **rate of unemployment**. The measurement of people without jobs who are actively seeking work is very difficult to determine. A number of methods for measuring unemployment are used, each with its own flaws and advantages. The comparison of unemployment between different countries is very inaccurate due to different definitions of unemployment and different social structures of countries. Unemployment has significant costs to both an economy and society but also provides some economic benefits. Depending on the perspective taken, unemployment at various levels will affect an economy in different ways. More conservative economists argue that the marketplace will determine unemployment, while welfare economists call for government action in the field.

Costs

Unemployment has both **social and economic costs** to individuals and society. The psychological impact of being unemployed degrades self-esteem, creates a sense of purposelessness, and increases mental strain. The financial implications can impair family life, reduce the standard of living, and make it difficult for some to receive benefits such as health insurance and disability payments, which are often part of an employment package. When workers are unable to find appropriate positions for their level of training and education, they are sometimes forced to take inferior jobs. These individuals are said to be underemployed and are generally dissatisfied members of the workforce. High unemployment has profound economic costs in many situations. It typically reflects low GDP, which implies both inefficient use of resources and the failure of production to provide products that improve the general welfare.

Benefits

The major benefit of unemployment is that it has a **"cooling" effect** on the economy and tends to **restrict general inflation**. Many economists feel that given the scarcity of natural resources and the environmental pollution associated with rapid economic growth, it is not possible to continue increasing GDP year after year. Unemployment is a restraint to such growth. Welfare economists argue the burdens of slowing the economy should not fall on the poorest and least able to cope members of society. They believe improved technology and planned economic growth that considers environmental factors will allow modest, healthy growth with low unemployment. In any economy, there are a certain number of members of the workforce moving from job to job and seeking work they consider more appropriate to their skills. This common type of unemployment is termed **frictional unemployment**.

Types

There are several types of unemployment recognized by economists. **Cyclical unemployment** results in recessionary periods of the business cycle when aggregate demand falls. When there is a major change in structure or skill level of an industry, unemployment may result. The advent of computers for word processing made typewriters virtually obsolete, causing those who make, sell, and repair typewriters to be unemployed. Changes in the market due to shifting demand for certain products affect the employees who produce those goods. If demand for typewriters falls, demand for the labor involved with typewriter production and sale also drops. This is also an example of unemployment caused by **technological advances**. Another type of unemployment is **seasonal unemployment**, where productive activity in an industry is limited to certain times of the year. Commercial harvesting of oysters is such a seasonal position.

Measurement in the United States

Measuring unemployment in the United States is done with statistics and data obtained by the **US Bureau of Labor Statistics**. Most countries have a similar agency providing this service. The major criterion for determining if an individual was gainfully employed during the weekly measuring period is straightforward. People are deemed to have been employed if they did any activity for pay or profit during the period. Included in this group are temporary workers and seasonal employees. Included in this calculation of employment are those who do hold jobs but were unable to work because of personal obligations, holidays, sickness, labor strikes or lock-outs, inclement weather, or temporary maternity or paternity reasons. Homemakers, students, and those imprisoned are excluded from the calculation of the employed. Individuals are classified as unemployed if they have actively sought work in the previous month and are ready and able to be employed.

Recessions

The technical definition of a **recession** is when a nation's real Gross Domestic Product decreases in two or more consecutive quarters of the fiscal year. Typically, recessions involve falling aggregate demand, which causes prices to fall and economic activity to slow. It sometimes occurs when inflation rises quickly and is combined with a slowing economy. This condition is called "**stagflation**." In general, recessions are characterized by falling prices. Recessions appear in a more or less regular pattern in capitalistic economies. Recent patterns have indicated a recession may be expected every five to ten years. Most recessions are caused by lack of consumer and business confidence in the future. Some economists encourage government intervention in a recession, while others feel such interference only adds to the problem. The latter group are more conservative economists who prefer to let the market determine the level of economic activity.

Depression in the United States

Only once has the United States gone through a massive **depression**. In the 1920s, massive speculation and investment in stocks caused their prices to rise far above their true value. Adding to the problem was the fact that many of the stocks were purchased on credit, using securities as collateral. When the economy began to contract, share prices fell dramatically and the collateral supporting other stock purchases became worthless. The loans were called, became uncollectible, and triggered a financial panic that led to multiple failures in the banking system. Savings were lost, unemployment soared, and the economy spiraled into a depression. After the election of **Franklin Roosevelt** in 1932, large amounts of money were injected into the economy. Precautions against future bank failures were addressed by federal insurance programs, and speculation in the stock market was regulated as well. Although these measures helped the economy, it was not until the United States entered World War II that it emerged from the effects of the depression.

Multiplier Effect

The multiplier effect is a theory that postulates that a single injection of funds into an economy may cause an effect far beyond what might be anticipated. The **multiplier effect** is an analytical tool favored by Keynesian economists to advance their theories of increasing aggregate demand. For example, a decision to build a new shopping center has a much bigger impact on the economy than indicated in the single transaction. Builders will be hired, retail stores will open, and restaurants and theatres may flourish, all creating jobs and income that far outweigh the initial investment in the shopping center. The multiplier effect is seen most clearly in economic situations where there are significant unused resources in the economy that may be engaged by an investment of capital. This investment is said to increase incomes, demand, and employment and give a general boost to the economy. Not all schools of economics recognize the multiplier effect equally, but it has become a standard tool in modern economics.

Accelerator Effect

The accelerator effect is a hypothetical theory that posits that the general economic condition will have a major impact on **private investment** in the economy. The sequence of events may occur as follows: as Gross Domestic Product rises, business confidence increases with the expectation of increasing sales, income, profit, and more efficient use of existing resources. The expansion spiral may continue as businesses increase investment and employment, and worker income and consumption also rise. The multiplier effect can accelerate all of these economic indicators, causing yet more expansion. The accelerator effect may also be seen in a contracting economy. As economic activity slows, businesses cut employment and investment in anticipation of reduced profits. These effects are all accelerated and the downward spiral of the economy is exacerbated. If unchecked, this deflationary spiral may lead to a **recession**, or in the worst case, a **depression**.

Economic Cycles

Cycles of expansion and contraction of economic activity seen regularly in economies are called **business (or economic) cycles**. The expansion or contraction tends to occur across the board in almost all areas of economic activity, contributing to the impact and intensified by the accelerator concept. Standard measurements of economic activity are increases or decreases in the **real Gross Domestic Product**. Although there are definite patterns of economic cycles, they cannot be predicted accurately because of multiple factors affecting the economy. Cycles tend to have their own lifespan, and there is a debate as to whether government interventions are useful in smoothing out the fluctuations. The **prediction of economic cycles** has become a major factor in business, social, and political arenas.

Green Economics

Green economics is a general term that includes economics as one part of the total ecological system. It is an interdisciplinary branch of economics, including contributions from the social sciences, biology, and economics. **Green economics** should be thought of as a loose confederation of movements, ideas, schools, and theorists, rather than a single solid school of thought. A general mission statement for green economics is that the economy is one element in the **ecosystem**, and the ecosystem plays an important role in economic decisions. The concept of scarce resources is central to green economics, as is the idea of sustainable resources. Given the agreement that all resources are limited in a sense, green economics advocates moderate economic growth, with ecologically sound principles that maintain rather than consume our limited resources.

Government Debt in Depth

Any obligation owed by local, state, or federal governments is considered **government debt**. Such a debt is actually an indirect debt of the taxpayers as a whole, though it is seldom understood this way. Debt is most often incurred by issuing securities, primarily bonds, with varying lengths of maturity. Debt that is owed to citizens of the country incurring the obligation, is known as **internal debt**. However, debt held by individuals, institutions, and governments from another country is called **external debt**. Although the great majority of government debt is incurred by notes and bonds, some governments may borrow from central or commercial banks. Fiscal conservatives rail against public debt while more liberal economists and politicians support raising funds for social welfare and defense. The issue of United States public debt, also called the **deficit**, has become an issue in politics and welfare economics.

Economic Models

In economics, as in other disciplines, **models** are constructed simulations of actual problems in order to test a set of variables. Models provide a framework that clearly illustrates the change in economic elements when different variables are applied. In economics, a model is a theoretical construct that represents economic processes by a set of variables and a set of logical and quantitative relationships between them. As in other fields, models are simplified frameworks designed to illuminate complex processes. Economic models are widely used in academic settings and in economic research. Businesses use economic models to plan and allocate resources, as well as predict the impact of economic actions. Governments use models of the economy to plan policies and justify the implementation of economic decisions. Models are also useful in predicting future economic activity.

Econometrics

A collection of mathematical and statistical tools used in advanced economic theory are given the general name of **econometrics**. Econometrics is used extensively in economic research and in the creation of economic models. Econometrics allows researchers to place numerical values on economic concepts and verify posited hypotheses. An example of a widely used econometric formula is regression analysis. When econometrics is used to study a variable over a specified span of time it is referred to as a **time-series analysis**. An example would be the impact of savings in a business cycle for the past 30 years. When econometrics is employed to measure different variables at one point in time, it is termed **cross-sectional analysis**. Both time-series and cross-sectional analyses are used extensively in economic modeling.

Definitions Used for Macroeconomics of the Labor Market

Macroeconomics of the labor market starts with a series of definitions calculated from labor statistics:

- The **labor force** includes all people in an economy who have jobs or are actively seeking employment.
- To find the **participation rate** of individuals in the workforce, the aggregate number of the labor pool is divided by the size of the total population.
- The **unemployment rate** is calculated as a percentage of those who are unemployed but seeking jobs relative to the total population.

From these basic definitions, we can obtain **stock variables**, which measure a level at a particular point in time. **Flow variables**, on the other hand, are used to measure a variable over a specified period of time. Examples of flow variables include modifications of the labor market due to net entries and exits from the labor pool. This would include retirees, net immigration of eligible laborers, forced unemployment, and frictional unemployment. These are flow variables that may be studied over any length of time.

Balance of Payments

The measurement of a nation's **trade productivity** is the net of the imports and exports of finances, services, and finished goods in international trade with other countries. Financial capital and transfer payments also enter into the calculation. Each country has three accounts to measure international trade activity. The **current account** of a country has three components: the transfer account (for unilateral transfers), the income account (measuring net income received from international transactions), and the trade account (a record of goods and survives traded abroad). The **capital account** indicates the net gain or loss in capital obtained from international trade. This is primarily used for cash and financial paper, including loans, investments, and savings. Finally, the **unilateral transfer account** notes all transfers of asset for which there is no compensation. Each account may either have a surplus indicating the country gained more than they lost in that account, or a deficit noting the net loss for the country. The net total of all accounts gives a balance of payments figure for that period.

Okun's Law

Arthur Okun, an American economist, noted that changing unemployment rates had a significant impact on real GDP. **Okun's Law** seeks to describe this relationship. It may be summarized by stating each percentage drop in the unemployment rate results in a disproportionate rise in real GDP for the period measured. This observation made by Okun is based on observable empirical evidence rather than on extensive economic research and econometrics. The generally accepted ratio of Okun's Law is that for every one percent of increased employment there is a corresponding increase in real GDPof two to four percent. The significance of Okun's Law is the importance of increased employment in generating national wealth. It is often used to support economic policy which seeks to reduce unemployment and thus boost real GDP.

Macroeconomic Models

A macroeconomic model is a simulation of the forces in a macro-economy. Such models serve primarily to better understand the relationships under different variables of such macroeconomic measurements as total production, price behavior, level of employment of available resources, and total earned income. These models are used to set up hypothetical economic situations that test the effect of economic action on other variables in the model. Primarily used for forecasting future economic conditions, they are used in economic research at academic institutions, government agencies and institutions, and independent economic consulting groups. The first **macroeconomic models** were developed after World War II in Holland and the United States. A global macroeconomic model was conceived by economist Lawrence Klein, who was awarded the Nobel Prize in Economics for his work.

Laffer Curve

An important economic tool is called the **Laffer Curve**, which posits that governments may maximize tax revenue by setting tax rates at the apex of this curve and that any additional taxation actually reduces tax revenues. Developed by the economist **Arthur Laffer**, it is often used to justify tax-cutting policies popular with conservative and supply-side economists. The concept may be clarified by examining the extremes of zero taxation and a 100% tax rate. At zero taxation, the government receives no tax revenue at all. At 100% tax rates, the government also receives no tax revenue, because there is no economic incentive to work if all earned monies are collected as taxes. At some point between the two extremes is the tax rate that will secure the maximum revenue through tax receipts. Much of this is economic theory not proved in the real economic world. The curve will also vary from country to country due to different economic environments, which may skew the Laffer curve in unpredictable ways.

Economic Language and Reasoning

The methodology of economics is not unlike other sciences. The first step is the collection of **observed economic information** collected without bias. These observations ideally have measurable values that give a measure of worth. This information is collected and used in the creation of **economic models** illustrating relationships between economic variables. Examples of such relationships include price levels to consumption, and unemployment and national income. These models may be simple organizational tools for data or complex calculations of relationships between dynamic economic factors. Finally, taking the organized observed data and constructing a model, generation of **economic statistics** should follow. These statistics will be drawn from a simulated economy or economic situation and may measure the impact of an economic action on all other variables in the model. This will provide the basis for making informed economic decisions from information gained in the simulation.

Economic Policy

Economic policy refers to the broad planning and implementation of economic measures of the government in regulating and affecting economic activity. It includes wide areas of monetary and fiscal policy, and affects virtually every aspect of an economic system. Politics and social pressures play a major role in influencing **economic policy**. International agencies and institutions such as the World Bank may also play a part in determining economic policy. Several general areas of economic policy may be identified:

- **Fiscal policy and stance** refers to the government deficit or surplus and the methods of financing government operations.
- Policies on **taxation** include changing tax regulations, enforcing tax codes, and the methodology of tax collection.
- **Government spending** for usual operations of the government and special allocations for natural disasters and war.
- Determining the amount of money in **circulation**.
- The determination of **interest rates** that fall under government control.
- **International trade policy** including tariffs, reciprocal trade arrangements, and trade treaties.
- The rules and regulations that apply to the **banking system**.

Stabilization Policy

Economic stabilization may refer to two different things which require different policy and economic action. One area of **stabilization** that is common is the smoothing out of the business cycles to avoid extremes. This type of policy goal may be attained by a combination of monetary and fiscal policy in order to minimize economic fluctuations and avoid inflation or recession. Usually, the actions implemented are counter-cyclical, balancing economic trends with a goal of a stable economy. Occasionally, an unexpected economic crisis arises which demands immediate government action. Perhaps a trauma to the banking or securities markets has caused a short-term situation that requires government intervention to ease the situation. In these cases, both the government and central bank work together to remedy the situation, sometimes with the help of international economic agencies.

Fiscal Policy

Fiscal policy is the collection of money by the government to finance operating expenses and unilateral transfer payments to its citizens. The money is also used for social services and programs to maintain and improve the infrastructure of the country. The primary means of raising funds are collecting taxes from individuals and businesses, borrowing by issuing notes and bonds, and taxing services. **Fiscal policy** can be used to prime the economy by injecting funds into the system in order to increase aggregate demand. Governments must pay interest on the bonds and bills they issue to raise funds. The maturity dates vary widely between short-term treasury bills and longer-term US bonds. Monies paid as interest are raised primarily by taxation. Total net government debt is called the **deficit** and remains an issue of controversy for economists and politicians alike. This debt should be devalued by the country's inflation rate to reflect an accurate figure.

Internal Economic Stabilizers

The economy has some built-in **stabilizers** to help smooth out the business cycles. Both tax revenue and transfer payments adjust automatically when the economy begins to contract. **Income tax revenues** fall because of a decrease in employment. **Transfer payments** increase as individuals use food stamps and other government aid programs to bolster their income. This means that net disposable income is not totally dependent on the economy's level of production, and the transfer payments allow more consumption to occur than might be anticipated. Safeguards are also built in the banking system by federal insurance programs, and the stock market operates with rules and regulations imposed to prevent another panic similar to the 1929 crash. The entire economy has become more stable as a result of government policy intended to avoid the extremes in the economic cycle.

Government Intervention in Price Levels

Governments may manipulate price levels in a number of direct and indirect ways. They can directly affect levels by imposing price ceilings or price floors, limiting the range of price fluctuations of a good or service. Rent controls are an example of **price ceilings** city governments impose on landlords in some metropolitan areas. The classic example of **price floors** is the minimum wage requirements for labor in some economies. Governments may also affect aggregate demand and supply by different policies and intervention. Keynesian economists believe the government is responsible for increasing aggregate demand in a contracting economy. Monetary theorists believe the level of economic activity is directly linked to the total supply of money in the economy and use monetary and fiscal policy to determine the increase or decrease in the money supply, and thus the level of prices. **Subsidies** are another means the government may use to artificially manipulate prices in an economy.

Aggregate Demand, Supply, and Equilibrium Output

The equilibrium level of aggregate supply and aggregate demand in macroeconomics is the **equilibrium output**. The level of prices is an important determinant of equilibrium points. **Aggregate demand** reflects the total spending of individuals, businesses, and governments, as well as the net balance of payment accounts. The price level in macroeconomics determines total spending because of its impact on interest rates, the amount of wealth in the economy, and the international trade implications in price changes. Increases in prices will push up interest rates, which usually have a dampening effect on spending. The wealth of an economy decreases as prices fall, devaluing the assets in that society. Price changes can benefit a country whose prices remain stable, while their trading partners have a general increase in prices. Goods and services become cheaper to buy in the country with falling prices than in those with a stable price level. All of these factors work in concert to move an economy toward **equilibrium**.

Income Distribution and Social Welfare

Income distribution in an economy measures the patterns of the allocation of income among individuals and groups. In a sense, the **distribution of income** not only shows the income levels of individuals but also weights their relative importance in an economy. To calculate the aggregate satisfaction of the economy as a whole, the utility of each member must be measured. Any measure has subjective elements that cannot be mathematically represented in a welfare economics analysis. Such a utility-based measure treats everyone the same; there is no relative difference between a wealthy individual and a poor one. Only the satisfaction of each is measured in absolute terms. The **Maximum-Minimum function** argues that when the members of society who have the least wealth have the most relative welfare satisfaction, only then is the welfare function maximized. Any welfare policy or intervention should address those in the most need. Both of the above examples are extreme positions on **social welfare theory**. In the real world, policy usually falls somewhere in between the two.

History of the Regulations of International Commerce

When international trade began to flourish under **mercantilism**, countries protected themselves with high tariffs and restrictions on what and how goods might be traded. Over time, **free trade** was recognized as the most beneficial way to promote economic well-being. This concept has been honored over the years (with some exceptions), and free trade remains the prevailing attitude in commerce between nations. In the modern economic era, treaties and agreements among countries have resulted in a more rigidly regulated international trade environment. Free trade has historically favored nations with the strongest economies, and that remains the case today. The leading countries of the free world all advocate free trade, and developing nations have recognized the advantages in expanding their markets into the global economy. The future of free trade seems bright and bodes well for a growing international business climate.

FREE TRADE AND TRADE BARRIERS

The exchange of goods and services across international boundaries can be termed "**free trade**" only if the traded products are untaxed and no restrictions apply. **Trade barriers** of one kind or another or tariffs make free trade impossible and are a deterrent to commerce between nations. Trade barriers may include tariffs, limited amounts of a specific product that may be exported to a country, and other laws, restrictions, taxes, or regulations limiting the unfettered commerce between countries. Free trade is also promoted by economic policies that foster the movement of both labor and capital between countries. This climate of economic cooperation is needed to ensure a working economic relationship between trading partners. Regional trade agreements or treaties often outline the rules and regulations of commerce between nations. A country cedes some of its economic independence when engaging in free trade. There are costs as well as benefits that must be assessed.

HISTORICAL PERSPECTIVE ON FREE TRADE

Historically, free trade has been an opportunity for a country to open and develop new markets to improve its economies. **Free trade** was largely unknown until the 15th century, and had grown steadily (but not without problems) over the decades. England, with a strong manufacturing economy, was a leader in advocating unfettered commerce among countries. The theory of free trade was included in the economic works of Adam Smith and David Ricardo. Free trade has been a subject of contention over the years, with different political, social, and economic systems resisting the concept. **Protectionism**, the policy of protecting economies against competitive imports, has been the main argument against free trade. Newly developing economies use protectionism to ensure the success of their budding industries. As their economies mature and grow stronger, the pressure for new markets often makes free trade an attractive option.

Chapter Quiz

Ready to see how well you retained what you just read? Scan the QR code to go directly to the chapter quiz interface for this study guide. If you're using a computer, simply visit the online resources page at **mometrix.com/resources719/aepaeconomics** and click the Chapter Quizzes link.

Economic Inquiry Skills

Collecting Information and Organizing and Reporting Results

The first step of compiling data for useful implementation requires narrowing down on a **topic**. The student should first read background information to identify areas that are interesting or need further study and that the student does not have a strong opinion about. The research question should be identified, and the student should refer to general sources that can point to more specific information. When he or she begins to take notes, his or her information must be **organized** with a clear system to identify the source. Any information from outside sources must be acknowledged with **footnotes** or a **bibliography**. To gain more specific information about his or her topic, the student can then research bibliographies from general sources to narrow down on information pertinent to the topic at hand. He or she should draft a thesis statement that summarizes the main point of the research. This should lead to a working **outline** that incorporates all the ideas needed to support the main point in a logical order. A rough draft should incorporate the results of the research in the outlined order, with all citations clearly inserted. The paper should then be edited for clarity, style, flow, and content.

Formulating Research Questions or Hypotheses

Formulating research questions or hypotheses is the process of finding questions to answer that have not yet been asked. The first step in the process is reading **background information**. Knowing about a general topic and reading about how other people have addressed it helps identify areas that are well understood. Areas that are not as well understood may either be lightly addressed in the available literature or distinctly identified as a topic that is not well understood and deserves further study. Research questions or hypotheses may address such an unknown aspect, or they may focus on drawing parallels between similar, well-researched topics that have not been connected before. Students usually need practice in developing research questions that are of the appropriate scope so that they will find enough information to answer the question, yet not so much that they become overwhelmed. Hypotheses tend to be more specific than research questions.

Identifying Main Ideas in a Document

Main ideas in a paragraph are often found in the **topic sentence**, which is usually the first or second sentence in the paragraph. Every following sentence in the paragraph should relate to that initial information. Sometimes, the first or second sentence doesn't obviously set up the main idea. When that happens, each sentence in the paragraph should be read carefully to find the **common theme** between them all. This common theme is the main idea of the paragraph. Main ideas in an entire document can be found by analyzing the structure of the document. Frequently, the document begins with an introductory paragraph or abstract that will summarize the main ideas. Each paragraph often discusses one of the main ideas and contributes to the overall goal of the document. Some documents are divided up into chapters or sections, each of which discusses a main idea. The way that main ideas are described in a document (either in sentences, paragraphs, or chapters) depends on the length of the document.

Using Electronic Resources and Periodicals for Reference

Electronic resources are often the quickest, most convenient way to get background information on a topic. One of the particular strengths of **electronic resources** is that they can also provide primary-source multimedia video, audio, or other visual information on a topic that would not be accessible in print. Information available on the internet is not often carefully screened for accuracy or for bias, so choosing the **source** of electronic information is often very important. Electronic encyclopedias can provide excellent overview information, but publicly edited resources like Wikipedia are open to error, rapid change, incompleteness, or bias. Students should be made aware of the different types and reliabilities of electronic resources, and they should be taught how to distinguish between them. Electronic resources can often be too detailed and overwhelm students with irrelevant information. **Periodicals** provide current information on social science events, but they too must be screened for bias. Some amount of identifiable bias can actually be an important source of information, because it indicates prevailing culture and standards. Periodicals generally have tighter editorial standards than electronic resources, so completeness and overt errors are not usually as problematic. Periodicals can also provide primary-source information with interviews and photographs.

Using Encyclopedias, Bibliographies, or Almanacs for Social Science Research

Encyclopedias are ideal for getting background information on a topic. They provide an overview of the topic and link it to other concepts that can provide additional keywords, information, or subjects. They can help students narrow their topic by showing the subtopics within the overall topic and by relating it to other topics. **Encyclopedias** may sometimes prove to be more useful than the internet because they provide a clearly organized, concise overview of material. **Bibliographies** are bound collections of references to periodicals and books, organized by topic. Students can begin researching more efficiently after they identify a topic, look it up in a bibliography, and look up the references listed there. This provides a branching network of information a student can follow. A pitfall of bibliographies is that when in textbooks or other journal articles, the references in them are chosen to support the author's point of view and so may be limited in scope. **Almanacs** are volumes of facts published annually. They provide numerical information on just about every topic, and are organized by subject or geographic region. They are often helpful for supporting arguments made using other resources and do not provide any interpretation of their own.

Primary and Secondary Resources

Primary resources provide information about an event from the perspective of people who were present at the event. They might be letters, autobiographies, interviews, speeches, artworks, or anything created by people with first-hand experience. **Primary resources** are valuable because they provide not only facts about the event but also information about the surrounding circumstances; for example, a letter might provide commentary about how a political speech was received. The internet is a source of primary information, but care must be taken to evaluate the perspective of the website providing that information. Websites hosted by individuals or special-interest organizations are more likely to be biased than those hosted by public organizations, governments, educational institutions, or news associations. **Secondary resources** provide information about an event but were not written at the time the event occurred. They draw information from primary sources. Because secondary sources were written later, they have the added advantage of historical perspective, multiple points of view, or resultant outcomes. Newsmagazines that write about an event even a week after it occurred count as secondary sources. Secondary sources tend to analyze events more effectively or thoroughly than primary sources.

Review Video: Primary and Secondary Sources
Visit mometrix.com/academy and enter code: 383328

Organizing Information Chronologically and Analyzing the Sequence of Events

To organize information chronologically, each piece of information must be associated with a time or a date. Events are ordered according to the time or date at which they happened. In social sciences, chronological organization is the most straightforward way to arrange information, because it relies on a uniform, fixed scale—the passage of time. Information can also be organized based on any of the "who, what, when, where, why?" principles.

Analyzing the sequence of chronological events involves not only examining the event itself but the preceding and following events. This can put the event in question into perspective, showing how a certain thing might have happened based on preceding history. One large disadvantage of chronological organization is that it may not highlight important events clearly relative to less important events. Determining the relative importance of events depends more strongly on interpreting their relationships to neighboring events.

Recognizing Cause-and-Effect and Comparing Similarities and Differences

Cause-and-effect relationships are simply linkages between an event that happened (the **effect**) because of some other event (the **cause**). Effects are always chronologically ordered after causes. Effects can be found by asking why something happened or looking for information following words like *so, consequently, since, because, therefore, this led to, as a result*, and *thus*. Causes can also be found by asking what happened. **Comparing similarities and differences** involves mentally setting two concepts next to each other and then listing the ways they are the same and the ways they are different. The level of comparison varies by student level; for example, younger students may compare the physical characteristics of two animals while older students compare the themes of a book. Similarity/difference comparisons can be made by listing written descriptions in a point-by-point approach, or they can be done in several graphic ways. Venn diagrams are commonly used to organize information, showing non-overlapping clouds filled with information about the different characteristics of A and B, and the overlapping area shows ways in which A and B are the same. Idea maps using arrows and bubbles can also be developed to show these differences.

Distinguishing Between Fact and Opinion

Students easily recognize that **facts** are true statements that everyone agrees on, such as an object's name or a statement about a historical event. Students also recognize that **opinions** vary about matters of taste, such as preferences in food or music, that rely on people's interpretation of facts. Simple examples are easy to spot. **Fact-based passages** include certainty-grounded words like *is, did*, or *saw*. On the other hand, **passages containing opinions** often include words that indicate possibility rather than certainty, such as *would, should*, or *believe*. First-person verbs also indicate opinions, showing that one person is talking about his or her experience. Less clear are examples found in higher-level texts. For example, primary-source accounts of a Civil War battle might include facts ("*x* battle was fought today") and also opinions ("Union soldiers are not as brave as Confederate soldiers") that are not clearly written as such ("I believe Union soldiers..."). At the same time that students learn to interpret sources critically (Was the battle account written by a Southerner?), they should practice sifting fact from these types of opinion. Other examples where fact and opinion blend together are self-authored internet websites.

Review Video: Distinguishing Fact and Opinion
Visit mometrix.com/academy and enter code: 870899

Determining the Adequacy, Relevance, and Consistency of Information

Before information is sought, a list of **guiding questions** should be developed to help determine whether information found is adequate, relevant, and consistent. These questions should be based on the **research goals**, which should be laid out in an outline or concept map. For example, a student writing a report on Navajo social structure might begin with questions concerning the general lifestyle and location of Navajos and follow with questions about how Navajo society was organized. While researching his questions, he or she will come up with pieces of information. This information can be compared to his or her research questions to determine whether it is **relevant** to his or her report. Information from several sources should be compared to determine whether the information is **consistent**. Information that is **adequate** helps answer specific questions that are part of the research goals. Inadequate information for this particular student might be a statement such as "Navajos had a strong societal structure," because the student is probably seeking more specific information.

Drawing Conclusions and Making Generalizations About a Topic

Students reading about a topic will encounter different facts and opinions that contribute to their overall impression of the material. The student can critically examine the material by thinking about what facts have been included, how they have been presented, what they show, what they relate to outside the written material, and what the author's conclusion is. Students may agree or disagree with the author's conclusion, based on the student's interpretation of the facts the author presented. When working on a research project, a student's research questions will help him or her gather details that will enable him or her to **draw a conclusion** about the research material.

Generalizations are blanket statements that apply to a wide number of examples. They are similar to conclusions but do not have to summarize the information as completely as conclusions. Generalizations in reading material may be flagged by words such as *all, most, none, many, several, sometimes, often, never, overall,* or *in general.* Generalizations are often followed by supporting information consisting of a list of facts. Generalizations can refer to facts or the author's opinions, and they provide a valuable summary of the text overall.

Evaluating and Interpreting Maps

The **map legend** is an area that provides interpretation information such as the key, the scale, and how to interpret the map. The **key** is the area that defines symbols, abbreviations, and color schemes used on the map. Any feature identified on the map should be defined in the key. The **scale** is a feature of the map legend that tells how distance on the map relates to distance on the ground. It can either be presented mathematically in a ratio or visually with a line segment. For example, it could say that one inch on the map equals one foot on the ground, or it could show a line segment and tell how much distance on the map the line symbolizes. **Latitude** and **longitude** are often shown on maps to relate their area to the world. Latitude shows how far a location is north or south from Earth's equator, and longitude shows how far a location is east or west from Earth's prime meridian. Latitude runs from 90°N (North Pole) to 0° (equator) to 90°S (South Pole), and longitude runs 180°E (International Date Line) to 0° (prime meridian) to 180°W (International Date Line).

Review Video: Elements of a Map
Visit mometrix.com/academy and enter code: 437727

Popular Map Projections

- **Globe**: Earth's features are shown on a sphere. No distortion of distances, directions, or areas occurs.
- **Mercator**: Earth's features are projected onto a cylinder wrapped around a globe. This generates a rectangular map that is not distorted at the equator but is greatly distorted near the poles. Lines of latitude and longitude form a square grid.
- **Robinson**: Earth's features are projected onto an oval-looking map. Areas near the poles are truer to size than in the Mercator. Some distortion affects every point.

- **Orthographic**: Earth's features are shown on a circle, which is tangent to the globe at any point chosen by the mapmaker. This generates a circular, 3D-appearing map similar to how Earth is seen from space.
- **Conic maps**: This family of maps is drawn by projecting the globe's features onto a cone set onto the globe. Some distortion affects most points.
- **Polar maps**: The land around the poles has been projected onto a circle. This provides much less distortion of Antarctica and the land around the North Pole than other map types.

Cartographic Distortion and Its Influence on Map Projections

Cartographic distortion is the distortion caused by projecting a three-dimensional structure, in this case, Earth's surface, onto the two-dimensional surface of a map. Numerous map projections have been developed to minimize distortion, but the only way to eliminate distortion completely is to render Earth in three dimensions. Most map projections have minimal distortion in some location, usually the center, and the distortion becomes greater close to the edges of the map. Some map projections try to compromise and distribute the distortion more evenly across the map. Different categories of maps preserve, or do not distort, different features. Maps that preserve directions accurately are **azimuthal**, and maps that preserve shapes properly are **conformal**. Area-preserving maps are called **equal-area maps**, and maps that preserve distance are called **distance-preserving**. Maps that preserve the shortest routes are **gnomonic projections**.

Review Video: Map Projections
Visit mometrix.com/academy and enter code: 327303

Comparing Maps of the Same Place from Different Time Periods

Maps of the same place from different time periods can often be initially aligned by **geographic features**. Political and land-use boundaries are most likely to change between time periods, whereas locations of waterways and geologic features such as mountains are relatively constant. Once geographic features have been used to align maps, they can be compared side-by-side to examine the changing locations of human settlement, smaller waterways, etc. This kind of map interpretation, at the smallest scale, provides information about how small groups of humans **interact with their environment**. For example, such analysis might show that major cities began around ports and then moved inland as modes of transportation, like railroads and cars, became more common. Lands that were initially used for agriculture might become incorporated into a nearby city as the population grows. This kind of map analysis can also show the evolution of the **socio-economics** of an area, providing information about the relative importance of economic activities (manufacturing, agriculture, or trade) and even the commuting behavior of workers.

Natural, Political, and Cultural Features on Maps

Map legends will provide information about the types of natural, political, or cultural features on a map. Some maps show only one of these three features. **Natural features** such as waterways, wetlands, beaches, deserts, mountains, highlands, and plains can be compared between regions by type, number, distribution, or any other physical characteristic. **Political features** such as state and county divisions or roads and railroads can be compared numerically, but examining their geographic distribution may be more informative. This provides information on settlement density and population. In addition, road and railroad density may show regions of intense urbanization, agricultural regions, or industrial centers. **Cultural features** may include roads and railroads, but might also include historic areas, museums, archaeological digs, early settlements, and even campgrounds. Comparing and contrasting the number, distribution, and types of these features may provide information on the history of an area, the duration of settlement of an area, or the current use of the area (for example, many museums are found in current-day cultural centers).

Comparing Maps with Datasets or Texts

Maps can provide a great deal of information about an area by showing specific locations where certain types of settlement, land use, or population growth occurred. **Datasets** and **texts** can provide more specific information about events that might only otherwise be hypothesized from maps. This specific information may provide dates of significant events (for example, the date of a fire that gutted a downtown region, forcing suburban development) or important numerical data (e.g., population growth by year). Written datasets and texts enable map interpretation to become concrete and allow observed trends to be linked with specific causes ("Real estate prices rose in 2004, causing middle-class citizens to move northwest of the city"). Without specific information from additional sources, inferences drawn from maps cannot be put in **context** and interpreted in more than a vague way.

Evaluating and Interpreting Other Graphic Formats

The type of information being conveyed guides the choice of **format**. Textual information and numeric information must be displayed with different techniques. Text-only information may be most easily summarized in a diagram or a timeline. If the text includes numeric information, it may be converted into a chart that shows the size of groups, connects ideas in a table or graphic, or shows information in a hybridized format. Numeric information is often most helpfully presented in tables or graphs. When information will be referred to and looked up again and again, tables are often most helpful for the reader. When the trends in the numeric information are more important than the numbers themselves, graphs are often the best choice. Information that is linked to the land and has a spatial component is best conveyed using maps.

Interpreting Charts and Tables

Charts used in social science are a visual representation of data. They combine graphic and textual elements to convey information in a concise format. Often, **charts** divide the space up in blocks, which are filled with text and/or pictures to convey a point. Charts are often organized in tabular form, where blocks below a heading all have information in common. Charts also divide information into conceptual, non-numeric groups (for example, "favorite color"), which are then plotted against a numerical axis (e.g., "number of students"). Charts should be labeled in such a way that a reader can locate a point on the chart and then consult the surrounding axes or table headings to understand how it compares to other points. **Tables** are a type of chart that divides textual information into rows and columns. Each row and column represent a characteristic of the information. For example, a table might be used to convey demographic information. The first column would provide "year," and the second would provide "population." Reading across the rows, one could see that in the year 1966, the population of Middletown was 53,847. Tracking the columns would show how frequently the population was counted.

Interpret Graphs and Diagrams

Graphs are similar to charts, except that they graphically show numeric information on both axes. For example, a **graph** might show population through the years, with years on the *x* axis and population on the *y* axis. One advantage of graphs is that the population during the time in between censuses can be estimated by locating that point on the graph. Each axis should be labeled to allow the information to be interpreted correctly, and the graph should have an informative title.

Diagrams are usually drawings that show the progression of events. The drawings can be fairly schematic, as in a flow chart, or they can be quite detailed, as in a depiction of scenes from a battle. Diagrams usually have arrows connecting the events or boxes shown. Each event or box should be labeled to show what it represents. Diagrams are interpreted by following the progression along the arrows through all events.

Using Timelines in Social Science

Timelines are used to show the relationships between people, places, and events. They are ordered chronologically and usually are shown left-to-right or top-to-bottom. Each event on the **timeline** is associated with a date, which determines its location on the timeline. On electronic resources, timelines often contain hyperlinks associated with each event. Clicking on the event's hyperlink will open a page with more information about the event. **Cause-and-effect relationships** can be observed on timelines, which often show a key event and then resulting events following in close succession. These can be helpful for showing the order of events in time or the relationships between similar events. They help make the passage of time a concrete concept and show that large periods pass between some events, while other events cluster very closely.

Using Political Cartoons in Social Science Studies

Political cartoons are drawings that memorably convey an opinion. These opinions may be supportive or critical and may summarize a series of events or pose a fictional situation that summarizes an attitude. **Political cartoons** are, therefore, secondary sources of information that provide social and cultural context about events. Political cartoons may have captions that help describe the action or put it in context. They may also have dialogue, labels, or other recognizable cultural symbols. For example, Uncle Sam frequently appears in political cartoons to represent the United States government. Political cartoons frequently employ caricatures to call attention to a situation or a person. The nature of the caricature helps show the cartoonist's attitude toward the issue being portrayed. Every element of the cartoon is included to support the artist's point and should be considered in the cartoon's interpretation. When interpreting political cartoons, students should examine what issue is being discussed, what elements the artist chose to support his or her point, and what the message is. Considering who might agree or disagree with the cartoon is also helpful in determining the message of the cartoon.

Analyzing Artifacts

Artifacts, or everyday objects used by previous cultures, are useful for understanding life in those cultures. Students should first discover, or be provided with, a **description** of the item. This description should depict what time period the **artifact** was used in and what culture used it. From that description and/or from examination of the artifact, students should be able to discuss what the artifact is, what it is made of, its potential uses, and the people who likely used it. They should then be able to draw **conclusions** from all these pieces of evidence about life in that culture. For example, analysis of coins from an early American archaeological site might show that settlers brought coins with them, or that some classes of residents were wealthy, or that trade occurred with many different nations. The interpretation will vary depending on the circumstances surrounding the artifact. Students should consider these circumstances when drawing conclusions.

Chapter Quiz

Ready to see how well you retained what you just read? Scan the QR code to go directly to the chapter quiz interface for this study guide. If you're using a computer, simply visit the online resources page at **mometrix.com/resources719/aepaeconomics** and click the Chapter Quizzes link.

Consumer Economics

Essential Workplace Skills, Education, Training, and Skill Development

There are a number of basic skills that are necessary to succeed in the **workplace**, the most important of which are time management, communication skills, and an understanding of current technology. Some other essential job skills are adaptability, planning and organizing a variety of tasks, solving simple and complex problems, and working in a team. However, even though these skills are essential in any business setting, it is important to realize that very few people naturally use all of these skills effectively. The only way for an individual to develop all of the skills necessary to succeed in the workplace is by **improving** through skill development exercises and programs and by **learning** new skills through education and job training.

Responses to Positive and Negative Incentives

Positive incentives (such as praise, promotion, raises in pay or allowance, or bonuses) can be extremely effective at encouraging a particular response. Individuals who are given **positive incentives** will be more willing to make suggested changes than individuals who are given negative incentives. The major disadvantage of positive incentives is that individuals may start to expect the incentive whenever a particular task is carried out. **Negative incentives** (such as a reduction in pay, suspension, or termination), on the other hand, usually do not require the individual or organization to sacrifice anything. However, negative incentives often elicit negative responses and may embitter employees toward the organization.

Relationship between Risk and Return

Any individual, organization, or business that is considering a potential investment or business venture should take into account both the potential **risk** and the potential **return**. The potential risk of an investment or venture is the likelihood that the investment will offer some return to the individual, organization, or business versus the likelihood that the investment or venture will fail and the individual or organization will lose the investment. The potential return of an investment or venture is a measurement of how much monetary value can be obtained in a particular venture. It is important for an individual to assess both the risk and the return of a particular investment; the higher the risk associated with a particular investment, the higher the potential return must be for the investment or venture to be worthwhile.

Investment and Credit

Investment is committing financial resources to a particular account or asset in order to earn a return at a later time. Each type of **investment** carries a different level of risk and a different potential return, though it can be difficult to determine exactly how profitable a particular endeavor will be in the long run. **Credit** is the process by which a financial institution lends funds to an individual for the purchase of a particular product or service. This means that the financial institution will cover the cost of the product or service in exchange for the individual agreeing to pay back that money, and any interest associated with the loan or credit, at a later time.

Savings and Investment Options

Savings and investment options include checking accounts, savings accounts, CDs (certificates of deposit), stocks, bonds, and mutual funds. The major advantage of investing in savings accounts, checking accounts, CDs, and bonds is that these investments are not risky, though the returns associated with these investments are usually low as well. CDs and bonds have a somewhat higher return than savings and checking accounts, but the money earned by the CD or bond, as well as the initial investment, can only be cashed out at certain times. Mutual funds are somewhat riskier than CDs or bonds, but the risk is still small, because mutual funds contain a diverse stock portfolio. Mutual funds usually yield significantly higher potential returns than standard checking and savings accounts. Stocks vary greatly in both risk and return.

Checking and Savings Accounts and CDs

Checking and savings accounts are two investment services offered by banks and other financial institutions as a way of protecting an individual's money while also providing a return on the deposit. The bank or other financial institution usually offers a small amount of annual interest on the account in exchange for the right to use that money for lending purposes. **Savings accounts** usually receive a reasonable amount of interest, while **checking accounts** usually accrue less interest than a savings account, if the account earns any interest at all. Financial institutions may also offer **CDs**, that pay higher interest rates. Funds are deposited in a CD for a set term and cannot be removed by the owner without penalty until the term limit is reached.

Stocks, Bonds, and Mutual Funds

A **stock** is an investment in which an individual purchases partial ownership in a corporation. Each stock certificate, or share, represents an equal amount of ownership in that corporation and allows the individual to share in the corporation's decision-making, to earn dividends from company profits, and to sell the stock at a later time. A **bond** is similar to a loan; the individual purchasing the bond is actually loaning his or her money to the institution for a set amount of time. In exchange for the loan, the institution agrees to pay back the principal and the interest associated with the loan when the amount of time set by the bond expires. A **mutual fund** is an investment in a variety of stocks, bonds, and other investment options in the hope of offering some return to each investor. Investors give money to a fund manager, who does his or her best to pick a list of safe and remunerative investments.

Important Factors for Comparing Financial Institutions

A person selecting a financial institution may want to start by determining his or her **needs** (checking accounts, savings accounts, CDs, safe deposit boxes, loans, etc.). The person may then want to consider the **fees** associated with each account, the minimum balance required for each account, and the amount of annual interest. Each financial institution has its own distinct fees and interest rates for each type of account. It is also important for the individual to know if the FDIC or the NCUA **insures** that particular financial institution; uninsured banks will not be able to guarantee deposits in the event of a financial emergency.

Spread Between Interest Earned and Interest Charged

Each financial institution has a **spread**, or difference, between the amount of interest an individual **earns** from an account and the amount of interest **charged** for loans and other services. The primary reason for the spread between the amount of interest earned and the amount charged is that banks and other financial institutions make their profit and cover their expenses with the interest they earn on loaning money that has been deposited. For example, say an individual deposits $50,000 into a savings account that earns 2% annually. The bank would then take a portion of that money and loan it to another individual at an interest rate of around 7%. The bank would then be able to pay the 2% promised to the depositor and keep the extra 4-5% that it charged the borrower to cover expenses, compensate for risk, and, hopefully, make a profit.

Simple and Compound Interest Rates

The appropriate amount of interest to be paid on a loan that uses **simple interest rates** can be determined by multiplying the principal (the total amount borrowed) by the simple interest rate for the period of the loan. For example, if an individual has a $10,000 loan with a 6% simple interest rate that must be paid off in one payment at the end of the year, the interest on the loan would be $600. A **compound interest rate**, on the other hand, bases the amount of interest for the loan on the sum of the principal of the loan and the total amount of interest accrued each time the loan is compounded. For example, if an individual has a $10,000 loan with 6% interest compounded semiannually, the interest the first time it compounds would be $10,000 × 6% = $600. The interest the second time it compounds would be $10,600 × 6% = $636, so the annual interest payment would be $600 + $636 = $1,236.

Review Video: Compound Interest Formula
Visit mometrix.com/academy and enter code: 100366

Creating a Personal Budget

A person planning a **personal budget** first should add up his or her annual income and cash on hand. Then, he or she should construct a list of all normal expenses, separating necessary expenses from luxury expenses. **Necessary expenses** are important to day-to-day survival and may include housing, food, utilities, transportation, and insurance. **Luxury expenses** are not necessary for survival, but rather improve quality of life; they include things like entertainment, jewelry, restaurants, and vacations. After adding up necessary expenses, the person should subtract that amount from his or her total annual income. The money left over from the annual income should then be budgeted for savings, and anything left after that for luxury expenses.

Factors That Affect an Individual's Credit Rating

An individual's credit score is determined by a number of factors, including payment history, length of time the individual has had credit with a particular institution, debt level, and ability to repay the loan. An individual's **payment history** primarily refers to whether or not his or her credit card and loan bills have consistently been paid on time, since this indicates to the lender that the individual will be able to pay back borrowed money. The individual's **level of debt** and **ability to pay back that debt** is extremely important in determining a credit rating. Each lender wants to make sure that the borrower will be able to earn enough money to repay all of his or her debt, and people with a lot of debt may not be able to do so.

Costs and Benefits Associated with the Use of Credit

Before accepting credit, one should be aware of the costs and benefits. The major **costs** associated with credit include the actual amount of the loan that needs to be repaid, the interest on the loan, any annual or monthly fees associated with having the loan, fees charged for late payments, and any fees charged to initiate the loan. Any financial institution offering credit is required by law to disclose information regarding fees, so one should know exactly how much it will cost to initiate the credit agreement, what regular payments need to be made, and the cost of missing a payment. In spite of all of these concerns, credit can be extremely **useful**, because it enables an individual to purchase a product, such as a car or house, that he or she would be unable to afford all at once.

Consumer Decision-Making Process

A consumer who is deciding which product or service to purchase should begin by determining his or her **goals**. Once the consumer has an idea of the goal that he or she is attempting to achieve by purchasing the product or service, the consumer can **research** the products and services that will achieve that goal. An individual can conduct this research by asking other people for suggestions, searching online, or searching through magazine and newspaper advertisements. It is also important for the consumer to determine what sort of **problems** are associated with the relevant products and services. The consumer can then purchase the product that best suits his or her needs.

Practices to Avoid When Making a Purchasing Decision

A consumer should **avoid buying** based on peer pressure, being unwilling to ignore preconceived notions, and overgeneralizing. It is extremely important to gather information before making a purchasing decision; at the same time, consumers need to make their own decision without relying too heavily on peer influence. A consumer with preconceived ideas risks missing a better product. Finally, it is important to recognize the advantages and disadvantages of each product based on actual and practical information, rather than on the stereotypes and marketing hype surrounding a particular brand.

Techniques a Consumer Uses to Choose Group of Products and Services

Two of the most common techniques a consumer might use to evaluate a particular product are making a list of the advantages and disadvantages associated with a certain product and using a mathematical approach to evaluate a product. A **list of pros and cons** allows the consumer to determine which products best suit his or her needs and which products will be the most durable and reliable. When a purchase has the potential to save the consumer money, he or she might want to **calculate** the exact savings and the potential loss should the product fail.

Characteristics of Automobile Insurance

Automobile insurance transfers some of the financial risk associated with being in an automobile accident to an insurance provider in exchange for semiannual or annual premiums. There are six different types of **coverage**: bodily injury liability, collision, comprehensive, medical payments, property damage liability, and uninsured or underinsured motorist coverage. **Bodily injury liability** insures against the costs associated with other people being injured in an accident, **collision coverage** insures against the costs of repairing the consumer's automobile due to a collision with another object or automobile, and **comprehensive coverage** insures against the costs associated with replacing a stolen or damaged automobile. **Medical payment coverage** insures against the costs associated with injuries to individuals inside the consumer's vehicle, **property damage liability** covers damage to another owner's property, and **uninsured or underinsured motorist coverage** insures against the costs associated with accidents caused by an uninsured driver.

Characteristics of Health Insurance

Health insurance allows a consumer to transfer some of the financial risk associated with medical care to an insurance provider in exchange for a monthly premium. **Health insurance plans** cover a variety of different expenses, including visits to a physician, hospital stays, emergency room visits, surgical expenses, and medication costs. However, the precise medications and services covered vary from plan to plan; for instance, some plans only pay for the generic version of name-brand prescriptions and only cover the expenses associated with company-approved physicians and facilities. It is also possible that the insurance plan will only cover certain types of procedures and will only cover those procedures if certain conditions, such as the amount of time spent in the hospital, are met.

Characteristics of Disability Insurance

Disability insurance transfers some of the financial risk associated with illness or injury to an insurance provider in exchange for a monthly premium. This means that **disability insurance** will actually pay out a percentage of the consumer's income for any period that the consumer is unable to work due to disability. The exact amount paid out depends upon the plan, the consumer's amount of income, and the period that the consumer is out of work. The cost of purchasing disability insurance varies greatly and depends on the amount of income the insurance provider is required to insure. Consumers who are considering disability insurance should make sure they are not already receiving some form of coverage from their employer, as most states require employers to have some form of short-term disability coverage. Even if the consumer is covered, he or she may want to look into long-term coverage.

Characteristics of Property Insurance

Property insurance transfers some of the financial risk associated with destruction to the consumer's home to an insurance provider in exchange for an annual premium. There are several different types of **property insurance**, but the two primary types are homeowners insurance and renters insurance. **Homeowners insurance** is for individuals who actually own the unit or building; the insurance covers the building itself and any property inside. **Renters insurance**, on the other hand, is for consumers who rent the unit or building; the insurance covers anything inside the unit or building, but not the building itself. Some of the disasters that property insurance will usually cover are fire, smoke, lightning, hail, explosion, theft, vandalism, and damage caused by cars and other vehicles. Some of the disasters that property insurance will usually not cover are earthquake damage, flood damage, mold damage, and termite or other insect damage. However, additional coverage can be purchased to cover flood damage and earthquake damage.

Chapter Quiz

Ready to see how well you retained what you just read? Scan the QR code to go directly to the chapter quiz interface for this study guide. If you're using a computer, simply visit the online resources page at **mometrix.com/resources719/aepaeconomics** and click the Chapter Quizzes link.

AEPA Practice Test

Want to take this practice test in an online interactive format?
Check out the online resources page, which includes interactive practice questions and much more: **mometrix.com/resources719/aepaeconomics**

1. Assume a society has a given production possibilities frontier (PPF) representing the production of cheese and butter. Which of the following would cause the PPF to move outward?

a. The invention of a new machine that makes cheese more efficiently
b. An increase in the production of butter
c. An increase in the production of cheese
d. A decrease in the production of cheese and butter
e. An increase in the production of cheese and butter

2. Which of the following will result if two nations use the theory of comparative advantage when making decisions of which goods to produce and trade?

a. Each nation will make all of their own goods
b. Both nations will specialize in the production of the same specific goods
c. Each nation will specialize in the production of different specific goods
d. Neither nation will trade with one another
e. One nation will produce all goods for the other in addition to their own goods

3. What does the data in the following table most directly describe?

Inputs	1	2	3	4
Output	20	50	80	100

a. The Law of Diminishing Marginal Returns
b. Law of Increasing Opportunity Cost
c. Law of Demand
d. Consumer surplus
e. Marginal utility

4. Which of the following is NOT a part of the business cycle?

a. Expansion
b. Contraction
c. Recovery
d. Peak
e. Stagflation

5. Which of the following best defines American GDP?

a. The value, in American dollars, of all goods and services produced within American borders during one calendar year
b. The value, in American dollars, of all goods and services produced by American companies during one calendar year
c. The total value, in American dollars, of all American household incomes during one calendar year
d. The value, in American dollars, of a "market basket" of goods and services in one year divided by the value of the same market basket in a previous year multiplied by 100
e. The net value, in American dollars, of exports minus imports of the United States.

6. What must nominal GDP be multiplied by to arrive at real GDP?

a. GNP
b. CPI
c. Supply
d. Demand
e. A price deflator

7. Ivy loses her job because her skills as a seamstress are no longer required due to a new piece of machinery that does the work of a seamstress more quickly and for less money. Which type of unemployment is this?

a. Frictional
b. Structural
c. Cyclical
d. Careless
e. Technological

8. Which is considered part of the natural rate of unemployment?

I. Structural unemployment
II. Frictional unemployment
III. Cyclical unemployment

a. I only
b. II only
c. III only
d. I and II only
e. I, II, and III

9. Assume that aggregate demand is at AD_1 and the government borrows money and then spends that money in order to attempt to move aggregate demand to AD_3. According to the theory of "crowding out," where is AD likely to wind up?

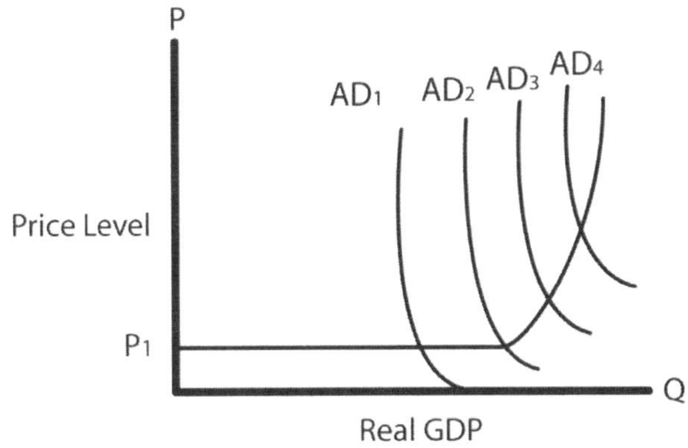

a. AD_1
b. AD_2
c. AD_3
d. AD_4
e. P_1

10. Which of the following statements about the long run aggregate supply (LRAS) curve is correct?

a. The horizontal part represents high levels of unemployment
b. The curved part represents high levels of unemployment
c. The vertical part represents high levels of unemployment
d. The LRAS curve is a straight, vertical line
e. The LRAS curve is a straight, horizontal line

11. Which of the following is a supply shock NOT likely to produce?

a. An increase in input prices
b. An increase in price levels
c. An increase in employment
d. A decrease in GDP
e. None of the above

12. How do banks create money?

a. By printing it
b. By taking it out of the Federal Reserve
c. By loaning it out
d. By putting it into the Federal Reserve
e. By taking out loans

13. Which of the following correctly states the equation of exchange?

a. $MV = PQ$
b. $MP \times VQ$
c. MP/VQ
d. $VP = MQ$
e. $1/MP = VQ$

14. John Maynard Keynes advocated what?

a. Supply-side economics
b. Demand-side economics
c. Laissez faire economics
d. The Laffer Curve
e. Say's Law

15. How is the long-run Phillips curve different than the short-run Phillips curve?

a. In the long-run Phillips curve, there is a trade-off between unemployment and inflation
b. In the long-run Phillips curve, unemployment is always greater than inflation
c. In the long-run Phillips curve, there is no trade-off between unemployment and inflation
d. In the long-run Phillips curve, unemployment equals inflation
e. In the long-run Phillips curve, there is no such thing as unemployment

16. The value of the goods and services exported by a country within a year and the goods and services imported by that same country during the same year is captured most directly in what?

a. Balance of payments
b. Current account
c. Capital account
d. Financial account
e. Trade account

17. An increase in the value of the American dollar in foreign exchange markets might be caused by what?

a. An increase in aggregate demand (AD) in the US
b. An increase in interest rates in the US
c. A balance of payments that equals zero (debits equal credits)
d. Inflation in the US
e. A decrease in interest rates in the US

18. A country's currency increases in value on foreign currency exchange markets. What will happen as a result?

I. Exports will drop
II. Imports will rise
III. The balance of payments will rise

a. I only
b. II only
c. I and II
d. II and III
e. III only

19. Which of the following are true of the demand curve?

I. It is normally downward sloping
II. It is normally upward sloping
III. It is influenced by the law of diminishing marginal utility
IV. It is unaffected by the law of diminishing marginal utility

a. I and III only
b. I and IV only
c. II and III only
d. II and IV only
e. IV only

20. Which of the following could best be used in order to determine the "price deflator" for converting nominal GDP to real GDP?

a. Consumer Price Index
b. Gross National Product
c. Business Cycle
d. Phillips Curve
e. Laffer Curve

21. Which of the following is correctly defined as the total of all currency, demand deposits, money market funds, saving accounts, and CDs under $100,000?

a. M0
b. M1
c. M2
d. M3
e. M4

22. Which of the following is a part, or component, of GDP?

a. GNP
b. Consumption
c. Supply
d. Demand
e. Elasticity of Demand

23. Which of the following would not cause aggregate supply (AS) to change?

a. An increase or decrease in land availability
b. The labor force suddenly increases dramatically
c. A new oil discovery causes dramatic decreases in power production
d. Worker productivity remains the same
e. A global pandemic keeps workers at home

24. Inflation has what effects?

a. Harms all members of an economy
b. Helps all members of an economy
c. Harms no members of an economy
d. Helps no members of an economy
e. Harms some members of an economy, helps others

25. Assume the Fed acts to try to keep rising prices stable. Which theory suggests that unemployment will increase as a result?

a. Phillips curve
b. Business cycle
c. Circular flow model
d. Classical economics
e. Rational expectations

26. A business takes out a one-year loan to pay for an investment on January 1. On December 31 of that year they pay the loan back. During that time, the nation experiences a recession, and the overall price level in the economy drops. Which of the following statements is true?

a. The nominal interest rate of the loan is greater than the real interest rate
b. The real interest rate of the loan is greater than the nominal interest rate
c. The nominal interest rate of the loan is greater than the nominal rate
d. The loan has a real interest rate but not a nominal rate
e. The loan has a nominal interest rate but not a real interest rate

27. Hyperinflation is most likely to be associated with:

a. Demand-pull inflation only
b. Cost-push inflation only
c. Demand-pull inflation and cost-push inflation
d. Peak-pull inflation only
e. Cost-push inflation and peak-pull inflation

28. The government increases spending by $1,000,000 and the multiplier is 5. How does this affect aggregate demand (AD)?

a. It has no effect
b. AD will increase by $5,000,000
c. AD will increase by $200,000
d. AD will decrease by $5,000,000
e. It is impossible to predict the effect

29. Assume that the loanable funds market is at equilibrium at the intersection of Id_{m1} and S. Then, the US government raises taxes on corporations. At which point is equilibrium established?

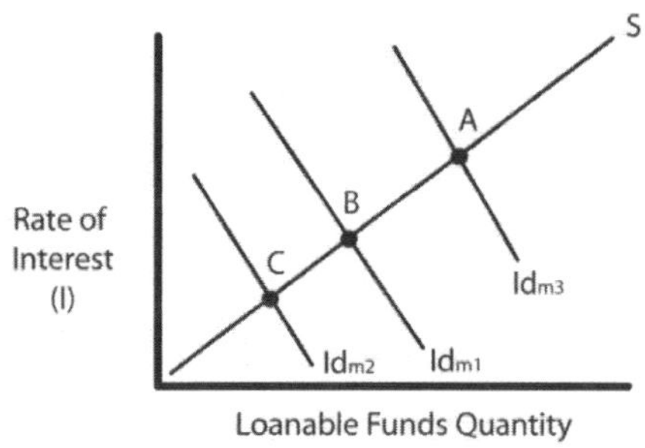

a. A
b. B
c. C
d. Some point above S
e. Between points A and B

30. The value of a "market basket" of goods and services in one year compared to the value of the same goods and services in another year is known as what?

a. CPI
b. GDP
c. GNP
d. CCI
e. DJI

31. Which of the following would NOT happen if the FOMC uses Treasury Bills to pursue a contractionary monetary policy?

a. The money supply decreases
b. The international value of the American dollar increases
c. The price of US goods to foreigners increases
d. American exports drop
e. Lower interest rates

32. The price of oil drops dramatically, saving soda pop manufacturers great amounts of money spent on making soda pop and delivering their product to market. Prices for soda pop, however, stay the same. This is an example of what?

a. Sticky prices
b. Sticky wages
c. The multiplier effect
d. Aggregate expenditure
e. Circular flow

33. Sally's grandmother has kept $100,000 in a cookie jar for years and then gave it to Sally, who immediately puts it in her bank in a savings account. The bank has a 20% reserve rate. Which of the following is true?

I. Excess reserves increase by $80,000
II. The money supply increases by as much as $120,000
III. Sally's grandmother earned money through inflation while she had the cash

a. I only
b. II only
c. I and II
d. III
e. I, II, and III

34. Assume that aggregate demand (AD) decreases. How will this decrease affect real GDP if there is a lot of unemployment as opposed to full employment?

a. If there is a lot of unemployment, prices will rise dramatically
b. If there is a lot of unemployment, GDP will stay the same
c. If there is full employment, GDP will increase dramatically
d. If there is full employment, prices will stay the same
e. If there is a lot of unemployment, GDP will decrease

35. Which of the following is most likely to benefit from inflation?

a. A bond investor who owns fixed-rate bonds
b. A retired widow with no income other than fixed Social Security payments
c. A person who has taken out a fixed-rate loan
d. A local bank who has loaned money out at fixed rate
e. A person who has stored cash savings at home, not in a bank account

36. How does unionized labor in an industry typically affect the wages of workers in that industry during a downturn in the economy when AD decreases?

a. It makes wages more likely to decrease
b. It makes wages more "sticky"
c. It has no effect on wages; instead, it causes AS to decrease
d. It has no effect on wages; instead, it causes AS to increase
e. It makes wages more likely to increase

37. Assume a nation's economy is in recession. The nation has an MPC of 0.9 and the government wants to enact fiscal policy to shift the AD curve by $10 billion dollars. What must the government do to its current spending rate?

a. Decrease spending by $10 billion
b. Increase spending by $10 billion
c. Decrease spending by $1 billion
d. Increase spending by $1 billion
e. Increase spending by $20 billion

38. Assume that Guatemala has a surplus in its capital account. What might this mean?

a. It must also have a surplus in its current account
b. The value of Guatemalan goods bought by foreigners is greater than the value of foreign goods bought by Guatemalans
c. Its balance of payments must be unequal
d. The value of foreign goods bought by Guatemalans is greater than the value of Guatemalan goods bought by foreigners
e. The trade account is balanced

39. The price of gasoline skyrockets, dramatically affecting the amount that producers spend to send their goods to market. What do you expect to happen in the short run?

a. Prices increase, GDP increases
b. Prices decrease, GDP decreases
c. Prices increase, GDP decreases
d. Prices decrease, GDP increases
e. Prices stay the same, GDP stays the same

40. A society produces 10 units of Good X and 10 units of Good Y. Then, the society changes its production, increasing production of Good X to 15 units. Production of Good Y drops to 6 units. What is the opportunity cost of producing the additional 5 units of Good X?

a. 5 units of Good X
b. 15 units of Good X
c. 6 units of Good Y
d. 4 units of Good Y
e. 5 units of Good X and 4 units of Good Y

41. Which of the following would be included in GDP?

a. The value of illegal drugs sold in a nation
b. Aluminum used to make airplanes
c. Lawn care provided by a professional nursery service
d. Computer chips used in Apple computers
e. Plastic used to make product packaging

42. In economic terms, which of the following is considered investment?

a. Buying a new home computer
b. Construction of a new manufacturing plant
c. Purchase of a college education
d. Selling finished goods to a customer
e. Purchasing raw materials for regular production

43. Which of the following would be most likely to try to combat inflation by decreasing the money supply?

a. A believer in the Laffer Curve
b. A supply-side economist
c. A Keynesian economist
d. An advocate of monetary policy
e. A believer in the Phillips Curve

44. Assume that the exchange rate between US dollars and Canadian dollars floats freely, and that American demand for Canadian dollars decreases. What is likely to happen?

a. Imports of American goods into Canada will increase
b. The price of Canadian dollars in terms of American dollars will increase
c. The price of US goods in Canadian dollars will decrease
d. The price of Canadian goods in American dollars will increase
e. The price of Canadian goods in American dollars will decrease

Refer to the following for question 45:

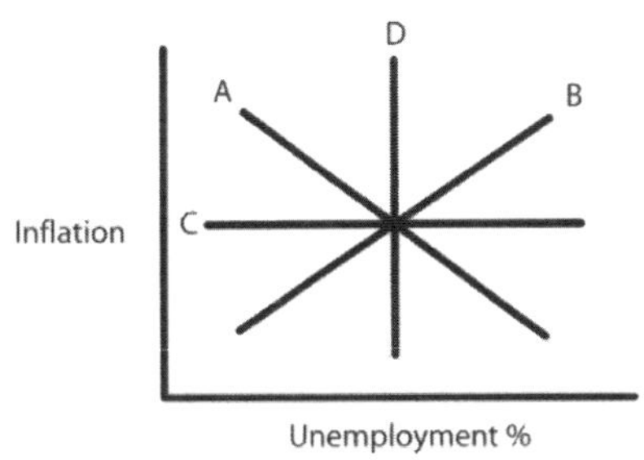

45. In the graph below, which curve (A, B, C, or D) represents the long-run Phillips curve?

a. A
b. B
c. C
d. D
e. Both A and B

46. Which of the following is included in the unemployment rate typically followed by economists?

I. Structural unemployment
II. Frictional unemployment
III. Cyclical unemployment

a. I only
b. II only
c. III only
d. I and II only
e. I, II, and III

47. Assume that the FOMC purchases bonds. Which of the following will happen?

a. The money supply increases, bond yields decline, bond interest rates decline
b. The money supply increases, bond yields increase, bond interest rates decline
c. The money supply increases, bond yields decline, bond interest rates increase
d. The money supply increases, bond yields increase, bond interest rates increase
e. The money supply declines, bond yields increase, bond interest rates increase

48. Which of the following statements is true of money?

I. It is necessary for trade
II. It is used in trade
III. It can make trade easier

a. I only
b. II only
c. III only
d. I and II only
e. II and III only

49. Cost-push inflation might be caused by:

I. A sudden, large increase in the cost of inputs used to make products
II. Total spending exceeding total productivity
III. Governments engaging in fiscal policy

a. I only
b. II only
c. III only
d. I, II, and III
e. II and III only

50. Which of the following is an element of the theory of rational expectations?

a. People have no rational reason to expect monetary and fiscal policy
b. Because people don't expect monetary and fiscal policy, they are caught unaware by it
c. Because people are caught unaware by monetary and fiscal policy, the effects of the policy are exaggerated
d. The lack of a rational reason to expect monetary and fiscal policy causes great swings from the natural rate of unemployment
e. People adjust their actions as a result of rational expectations of fiscal and monetary policy

51. Economics is best defined as the study of what?

a. Scarcity
b. Business
c. Trade
d. Supply and demand
e. Efficiency

52. According to Adam Smith, what brings about the maximum levels of production of goods and services when faced with limited resources?

a. Opportunity cost
b. Specialization
c. Inelastic demand
d. Monopolistic competition
e. Public subsidies

53. The price of fleece blankets goes up from $10 to $11. At the same time, demand goes down from 1,000 blankets to 800 blankets. Which of the following statements is true?

a. Demand is elastic
b. Demand is inelastic
c. The price elasticity quotient, or E_d, is less than 1
d. The price elasticity quotient, or E_d, is equal to 1
e. Demand is unitary elastic

54. Good A and Service B are complements. Which of the following is true?

a. An increase in price for Good A will lead to an increase in demand for Service B
b. A decrease in price for Good A will lead to decreased demand for Service B
c. An increase in demand for Good A will lead to increased revenues for providers of Service B
d. Demand for Good A will not affect demand for Service B
e. An increase in demand for Service B will lead to a surplus of Good A

55. Which of the following areas represents consumer surplus?

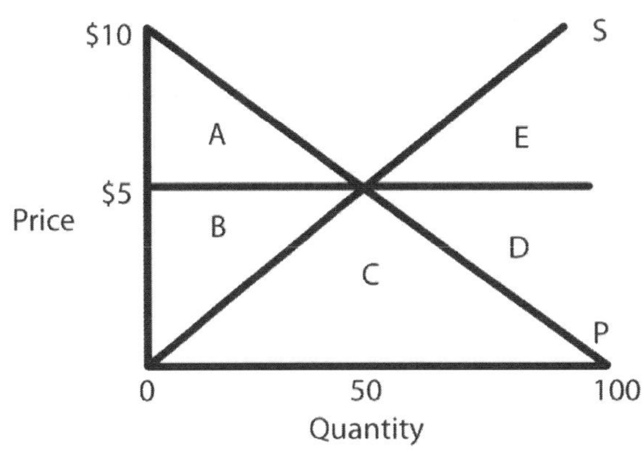

a. A
b. B
c. C
d. D
e. E

56. What would you expect to happen to marginal product as the number of inputs used is increased?

a. It will consistently increase
b. It will consistently decrease
c. It will decrease, stay constant, then increase
d. It will increase, stay constant, then decrease
e. It will stay the same

57. Consider the following data for a firm's use of labor input:

Input (Labor)	1	2	3	4	5
Product Output	10	30	40	45	47
Total Revenue	$10,000	$30,000	$40,000	$45,000	$47,000

What is the marginal product of labor of the 5th worker hired?

a. 2
b. 23.5
c. 47
d. 2,000
e. 47,000

58. When should a firm shut down in the short run?

I. If total costs are greater than total revenues
II. If total variable costs are greater than total revenues
III. If total fixed costs are greater than total revenues

a. I only
b. II only
c. III only
d. I and II only
e. I, II, and III

59. Which of the following is not true of monopolistic competition?

a. There are no great barriers to entry or exit from the market
b. Firms within monopolistic competition benefit from product differentiation
c. Firms within monopolistic competition maximize profit by producing where MR = MC
d. All or most firms within monopolistic competition attain long-run profit
e. Firms in monopolistic competition are efficient

60. You've invested $200,000 to start a new business, made revenues of $220,000, and had an opportunity to work for $40,000 during the same time. Which of the following is(are) true?

I. Accounting profit is $20,000
II. Economic loss is (-$20,000)
III. Opportunity cost of starting the new business is $240,000

a. I only
b. II only
c. III only
d. I and II only
e. I, II, and III

61. Which of the following statements is not true?

a. If the government imposes a tax on a good, the supply curve will shift to the left
b. If the government imposes a tax on a good, it will result in a deadweight loss
c. If the government imposes a tax on a good with a highly inelastic demand, it will be difficult for producers of the good to shift the cost to consumers
d. If the government imposes a tax on a good, the market price of the good will likely increase
e. If the government imposes a tax on a good, the demand for the good will likely decrease

62. The impact of a transaction on parties not directly involved in the transaction is known as what?

a. Social cost
b. Social benefit
c. Externality
d. Marginal social cost
e. Marginal social benefit

63. Which of the following is associated with market failure?

I. When a firm in a non-competitive industry hires labor at a lower wage
II. When the firms in a non-competitive industry create less than the efficient amount of a good or service
III. When production of a good creates negative externalities born by third parties
IV. Public goods

a. I and II only
b. II and III only
c. I and III only
d. I, II, and III only
e. I, II, III, and IV

64. What would you expect if a government price floor is established above the equilibrium price of a good?

a. Shortages of the good
b. Surpluses of the good
c. An increase in demand
d. A decrease in supply
e. Equilibrium price will decrease

65. Which of the market structures is most efficient?

a. Perfect competition
b. Monopolistic competition
c. Oligopoly
d. Monopoly
e. Collusive oligopoly

66. In general, cartels lead to which combination when compared with perfect competition?

a. High prices, increased production
b. Higher prices, lower production
c. Lower prices, higher production
d. Lower prices, lower production
e. Equilibrium of prices and production

67. How is a public good different than a private good?

I. Users cannot be excluded from using a public good.
II. The use of a public good by one person does not reduce the availability of that good for another person.
III. It is difficult to determine how much a user values a public good.

a. I only
b. II only
c. III only
d. I and II only
e. I, II, and III

68. A firm's long run average total cost curve is a curve that connects what?

a. The minimums of the firm's short run average total cost curves
b. The maximums of the firm's short run average total cost curves
c. The minimum of the firm's long run average total costs
d. The maximum of the firm's long run average total costs
e. All of the firm's different short run average total cost curves combined

69. What measures the impact of choosing one option over another?

a. Supply
b. Elasticity
c. Comparative advantage
d. The Law of Diminishing Marginal Returns
e. Opportunity cost

70. Ciao Bella Pizza faces this production function when making pizzas:

Pizzas Produced	Total Cost
0	0
1	6
2	12
3	18
4	23
5	28
6	32
7	37
8	43

Which pizza has the lowest marginal cost?

a. First
b. Third
c. Sixth
d. Seventh
e. Eighth

71. Thrifty Buy More sells blue baseball hats at $10 a hat in May. The equilibrium price for blue baseball hats increases to $12 in June. Which of the following is a potential explanation for the change?

a. An increase in supply of blue baseball hats
b. A decrease in demand for blue baseball hats
c. Both supply and demand stay the same
d. Government subsides make it less costly to produce blue hats
e. Substitute goods decrease in supply

72. Which of the following examples illustrates the law of diminishing marginal utility?

a. When the price of a good increases from $10 to $12, Bob demands less of the good
b. As the supply of a good increases, consumers demand less of the good
c. As Juan buys more units of a single good, he gets less satisfaction from each new purchase
d. As Sally's income decreases, she is forced to reconsider the goods and services she buys
e. As a consumer's income decreases, the total utility he or she derives from that income, measured in utils, also decreases

73. Assume you've invested $1,000,000 to begin a business. At the end of the year, revenues equal $1,200,000. During that same year, you could have worked for $300,000. Which of the following statements is true?

a. Accounting profit equals $200,000
b. Economic profit equals accounting profit
c. Accounting profit equals $300,000
d. Economic profit equals $500,000
e. The economic profit is greater than the accounting profit

74. What does the distinctive, outwardly bowed shape of the PPF signify?

a. The law of supply and demand
b. The efficiency of the free market system
c. That the two goods do not have constant opportunity costs when producing in different quantities along the PPF.
d. The unequal distribution of wealth within a society
e. The shift in demand to match a corresponding shift in supply

75. How will a labor union affect a labor market?

I. Increase supply of labor
II. Decrease supply of labor
III. Increase wage earned by labor
IV. Decrease wage earned by labor

a. I and III only
b. I and IV only
c. II and III only
d. II and IV only
e. I, II, and III

76. Firms will attempt to enter a market if the market is:

a. Operating where MR = MC
b. Operating where MC is greater than MR
c. Earning an accounting profit
d. Earning an economic profit
e. Earning a normal profit

77. In the long run, firms will exit a monopolistically competitive market when:

a. Profit is maximized
b. Price = marginal cost
c. Price exceeds marginal cost
d. There is an economic profit
e. Price is less than the minimum of the average total costs curve

78. Taxes, subsidies, price ceilings, price floors, taxes, and government regulations are all most commonly used for what purpose?

a. To correct market failure
b. To prevent the formation of trusts
c. To provide public goods
d. To prevent negative externalities
e. To promote an equal distribution of income

79. A company redevelops an old abandoned warehouse, creating an improvement to the neighborhood as a whole. This improvement to the neighborhood is known as what?

a. Private benefit
b. External benefit
c. Social benefit
d. Social cost
e. External cost

80. Which of the following is NOT true of a monopsonist or monopsony?

a. A monopsony is a market with just one buyer of a resource input
b. A monopsonist firm will hire additional labor until marginal revenue cost = marginal revenue product
c. A monopsonist faces a downward-sloping supply curve for labor
d. A monopsonist hires less than the efficient amount of labor
e. A monopsonist pays wages under the equilibrium wage rate

81. Proponents of legislating greater societal income equity, support all of the following:

I. Impose a progressive income tax
II. Impose high estate taxes
III. Impose a gift tax

a. I only
b. II only
c. III only
d. I, II, and III
e. II and III only

82. Assume that the equilibrium price for an apartment in Gotham City is $1,000 and the equilibrium quantity 10,000. Now, assume government steps in and creates a price ceiling at $850. Which of the following is likely to occur?

I. Demand will increase
II. Supply will increase
III. A price floor will also be established

a. I only
b. II only
c. III only
d. I and II only
e. II and III only

83. Assume the demand for a company's product is perfectly inelastic. Which of the following is true?

a. An increase in price will lead to a decrease in revenue
b. A decrease in price will lead to an increase in revenue
c. A decrease in price will increase demand
d. An increase in price will decrease demand
e. The demand curve would be vertical

84. How will the marginal revenue product curve of a firm in monopolistic industry compare with the marginal revenue product curve of a firm in a perfectly competitive industry?

a. The MRP curve for the monopolist will look the same as the MRP curve for the perfectly competitive industry
b. The MRP curve for the monopolist will slope upward, while the MRP curve for the perfectly competitive firm will slope downward
c. The MRP curve for the monopolist will slope downward, while the MRP curve for the perfectly competitive firm will slope upward
d. The MRP curve for the monopolist will slope downward, while the MRP curve for the perfectly competitive firm will be horizontal
e. The MRP curve for the monopolist will be horizontal, while the MRP curve for the perfectly competitive firm will slope downward

85. Which of the following statements concerning choice theory are correct?

I. Scarcity forces people, including producers, to make choices
II. Producers make choices and, as a result, face trade-offs
III. Opportunity cost is one way to measure the cost of a choice

a. I only
b. I and II only
c. II and III only
d. I, II, and III
e. III only

86. A determinant of demand increases. What follows?

I. The demand curve shifts to the right
II. The equilibrium price increases
III. The equilibrium quantity increases
IV. The supply curve shifts to the left

a. Only I
b. I and II only
c. I, II, and III only
d. I, II, III, and IV
e. None of the above

87. A company produces a good at a cost of $100. In doing so, it creates a certain level of pollution, unwanted by the neighborhood. The pollution is known as what?

a. Private benefit
b. Opportunity cost
c. Private cost
d. Social cost
e. External cost

88. Which of the following statements about price elasticity of supply is not correct?

a. If the percentage change in the quantity supplied is greater than the percentage change in price, the supply is elastic.
b. The supply of a good or service with a short life expectancy, such as fresh grapes, is inelastic.
c. Short-run supply for a factory producing a good through a complicated combination of resources tends to be inelastic.
d. Long-run supply for a factory tends to be more elastic than short-run supply.
e. If E_S is greater than 1, supply is inelastic.

89. The following table shows the marginal utility, measured in utils, that Kenny receives from purchasing good X and purchasing good Y. Good X costs $5, and good Y costs $10. Kenny has a total of $50 to spend on the two goods each week. If Kenny wants to maximize his total utility, which combination of goods should he buy?

Quantity of X	Marginal Utility of X	Quantity of Y	Marginal Utility of Y
1	8	1	20
2	6	2	12
3	5	3	8
4	4	4	6
5	3	5	4
6	2	6	3
7	2	7	3
8	2	8	2
9	1	9	2
10	1	10	1

a. 0 good X, 5 good Y
b. 2 good X, 4 good Y
c. 4 good X, 3 good Y
d. 6 good X, 2 good Y
e. 10 good X, 0 good Y

90. Which of the following is a role that the US federal government plays in the US economy?

I. Regulation of industries
II. Taxation
III. Provider of safety net for the poor
IV. Provider of public goods

a. I and II only
b. II and III only
c. II and IV only
d. I, II, and III only
e. I, II, III, and IV

91. Jasmine uses her income to maximize her total utility by buying 10 good A's and 5 good B's. Which of the following statements would be true if Jasmine got a raise, increasing her income by 10%?

a. Her buying behavior will not change
b. The marginal utility of good A will increase
c. The marginal utility of good B will increase
d. Her total utility, measured in utils, will increase
e. Her total utility, measured in utils, will decrease

92. Assume a business in a perfectly competitive market is operating such that marginal revenue equals marginal cost. Which of the following is true?

a. The firm will increase production
b. The firm will decrease production
c. The firm will continue producing at that quantity
d. The marginal profit of the next item produced will be positive
e. The marginal revenue from the next item produced will be greater than the marginal cost of that item

93. Which of the following statements is true about producer surplus?

a. It is always the same as consumer surplus
b. It is the part of the demand curve that reaches beyond the equilibrium point
c. A decrease in equilibrium price results in an increase in producer surplus
d. A decrease in equilibrium price results in a decrease in producer surplus
e. An increase in equilibrium price results in a decrease in producer surplus

94. A profit-maximizing monopolist will produce:

I. At a price higher than the minimum ATC
II. At a price lower than the minimum ATC
III. At an output above the demand of the demand curve and the marginal cost curve
IV. At an output below the intersection of the demand curve and the marginal cost curve

a. I and III only
b. I and IV only
c. II and III only
d. II and IV only
e. I, II, II and IV

95. Consider the following short-run data for Bob's Widgets, a perfectly competitive firm:

Total Revenue: $100
Total Costs: $200
Total Fixed Costs: $90
Total Variable Costs: $110

What should Bob's do?

a. Increase production
b. Decrease production but continue to produce
c. Lower fixed costs
d. Shut down
e. Lower prices

96. Which of the following statements about public goods is true?

a. The free market excels in producing them
b. When a person uses the good, it prevents others from using the good
c. There is no demand for public goods
d. It is difficult to prevent people from using the good without paying
e. They are equally valued by all people

97. Which of the following statements is true about an oligopoly?

a. There are no or very few barriers to entry
b. Many firms participate
c. Collusion may be planned or unplanned
d. The demand curve is straight
e. Economies of scale are limited or nonexistent

98. Short-run production is the time period during which ______. Long-run production is the time period during which ______.

a. a company's profits are maximized; a company's profits can be made greater
b. a company's costs are fixed; a company's costs can be decreased
c. a plant's revenue is fixed; a plant's revenue can increase
d. a company's production will not change; a company's production will change
e. a plant's production capacity cannot be changed; a plant's production capacity can be changed

99. Which basic questions do all economic systems need to answer?

I. Supply and demand
II. What goods and services will be produced?
III. How goods and services will be produced
IV. To which people will goods be distributed?

a. I only
b. I, II, and III
c. II and IV
d. II, III, and IV
e. IV only

100. Assume a company uses two inputs to produce a product. To determine the least-cost, profit-maximizing combination of inputs, what should the company do?

a. Use both inputs to the point where its marginal revenue product is greater than their price
b. Use both inputs to the point where their marginal revenue product is less than their price
c. Use both inputs to the point where their marginal revenue product is equal to their price
d. Use both inputs to the point where their marginal revenue product is highest
e. Use both inputs to the point where their marginal revenue product is lowest

Answer Key and Explanations

1. A: The production possibilities frontier shows the different possible combinations of goods (and/or services) a society can produce. If all other factors are even, producing more of Good A leads to a decreased production of Good B. If the PPF moves outward, that means a change in the factors of production that allows the economy to produce more goods—economic growth—has occurred. Something like innovation is an example of a cause of economic growth.

2. C: When a nation follows the theory of comparative advantage, it specializes in producing the goods and services it can make at a lower opportunity cost and then engages in trade to obtain other goods.

3. A: The input and output data illustrate the Law of Diminishing Marginal Returns, which states that as inputs are added during production, there eventually comes a time when increased inputs coincide with a decrease in marginal return.

4. E: The business cycle includes five stages: expansion, peak, contraction, trough, and recovery. Stagflation is the name for periods when inflation and unemployment are both increasing.

5. A: Answer B is a definition of gross national product (GNP), and answers C and D define other economic measures.

6. E: Nominal GDP is the total dollar value of goods and services produced in a country in a year. However, since prices increase with inflation, nominal GDP gives a skewed view of an economy when looking at various years over time. Therefore, economists multiply nominal GDP by a price deflator that accounts for inflation in order to arrive at real GDP.

7. B: Structural unemployment is unemployment that results from a mismatch of job skills or location. In this case, Ivy's job skill—her ability to work as a seamstress—is no longer desired by employers. Frictional and cyclical are other forms of unemployment; economists do not use the term careless unemployment.

8. D: It is believed that some level of frictional and structural unemployment will always exist, and that the best economists (and politicians) can hope for is to reduce cyclical unemployment to zero. Therefore, frictional and structural unemployment are sometimes referred to as natural unemployment, meaning unemployment that naturally exists within an economy.

9. B: According to the theory of crowding out, when the government borrows money to increase spending, this will increase the price of money, leading to a drop in investment. That drop in investment will have a negative effect on AD, and so the government injection of funds will not have its full, desired effect (AD_3), instead winding up at AD_2.

10. D: In the long run, aggregate supply does not depend on price. Aggregate supply in the long run depends strictly on the amount of capital and labor and the type of available technology.

11. C: A supply shock is caused when there is a dramatic increase in input prices. This causes an increase in price levels and decreases in employment and GDP. A supply shock causes the AS curve to move to the left (in).

12. C: Banks create money by giving out loans. For example, assume a person puts $100 into a bank. The bank will keep a percentage of that money in reserves because of the reserve requirement. If the reserve requirement is 10% then the bank will put $10 in reserves and then loan out $90 of it to a second person. The money total, which started at $100, now includes the original $100 plus the $90, or a total of $190. The bank creates $90 by loaning it.

13. A: The equation of exchange is MV = PQ. This means that M (a measure of the supply of money) multiplied by V (the velocity of money, or the average number of times a typical dollar is spent on final goods and services a year) is equal to P (the average price level of final goods and services in GDP) multiplied by Q (real output, or the quantity of goods and services in GDP).

14. B: John Maynard Keynes argued that government could help revitalize a recessionary economy by increasing government spending and therefore increasing aggregate demand. This is known as demand-side economics.

15. C: In the short-run Phillips curve, there is a trade-off between unemployment and inflation. There is no such trade-off in the long-run Phillips curve. According to the long-run Phillips curve, the economy tends to stay at the natural rate of unemployment, and any changes are minor variations that will self-correct.

16. B: The current account is part of what makes up a country's balance of payment account. The current account records the value of exports and imports of goods and services by a country, the country's net investment income, and the country's net transfers.

17. B: If interest rates in the US increase, foreign investors may send more money to the US. Those investors would have to first exchange their currencies for American dollars, making the American dollars more valued (scarce) and therefore increase in value.

18. C: If a country's currency increases in value, foreigners will have to give up more of their own currency to get the original country's currency in order to buy the original country's goods and services. This will cause a drop in exports. At the same time, it will be less expensive for people in the original country to exchange their currency for foreign currencies, causing the price of imported goods to drop and the total value of imports to rise.

19. A: As people have more and more of something, they value it less and less. This is the law of diminishing marginal utility, and it is what causes the downward slope of the demand curve.

20. A: Converting nominal GDP to real GDP requires some measure of the change in prices of goods and services within a nation over time. One could use the Consumer Price Index—the value of a fixed "market basket" of goods and services on a yearly basis—to determine the rate of inflation and then adjust nominal GDP to real GDP.

21. B: There are several different measures of the national money supply; these include M1, M2, and M3; there is no M4. M1 is defined as the total of all currency, demand deposits, money market funds, saving accounts, and CDs under $100,000.

22. B: The following is the equation for Gross Domestic Product:

$$\text{GDP} = \text{Consumption} + \text{Investment} + \text{Government Spending} + \overbrace{(\text{Exports} - \text{Imports})}^{\text{Net Exports}}$$

23. D: A change in productivity, such as workers becoming more or less productive, would affect how many goods can be supplied. No change in worker productivity would cause no change in AS. Choices A, B, and C would all affect input prices and therefore would all affect AS.

24. E: While rising prices may hurt many members of an economy, those same rising prices may benefit other members of the same economy. For example, rising prices may help those who sell goods and services and are able to keep their costs of production low, increasing their profit margin. Meanwhile, rising prices can hurt consumers because their income is now able to purchase fewer goods and services than before.

25. A: The Phillips Curve says that inflation and unemployment have an indirect relationship. If the Fed acts to stop inflation, then according to the Phillips Curve, unemployment will increase.

26. A: The nominal interest rate is stated interest rate, while the real interest rate is the nominal interest rate adjusted for inflation. If prices decrease during the period of the loan, the real interest rate will be less than the nominal interest rate.

27. A: Demand-pull inflation is caused when total spending is in excess of total production. This causes price levels to rise and can lead to hyperinflation.

28. B: The multiplier effect states that a given increase in spending, when multiplied by the multiplier, will lead to a given increase in AD. In this case, the $1,000,000 spending increase and the multiplier of 5 lead to an AD increase of $5,000,000 ($1,000,000 × 5 = $5,000,000).

29. C: When the government increases taxes on corporations, it lowers their willingness to invest—represented by the Id curve. That means that the Idm1 curve will move to Idm2, with a new equilibrium of C.

30. A: The Consumer Price Index is the value of a "market basket" of goods and services in one year compared to the value of the same goods and services in another year.

31. E: When the FOMC sells bonds, they raise interest rates. This draws money out of the American economy, and attracts foreign investors. This causes the value of the American dollar to rise overseas, which makes American goods more expensive to overseas buyers and causes American exports to drop.

32. A: The phenomenon of "sticky prices" refers to prices that stay the same even though it seems they should change (either increasing or decreasing).

33. A: Excess reserves will increase by $80,000, as the bank must keep 20% of the deposit, or $20,000, leaving $80,000. The money multiplier is 1/Reserve ratio, or 5, and that means the money supply could increase a total of $100,000 + (5 × $80,000) = $500,000. Because the cash was not able to earn interest, the cash decreased in value while it was stored in the jar.

34. E: When there is a lot of unemployment, the AS curve is horizontal. If AD decreases at this time, prices will tend to remain the same while GDP decreases. When there is full employment, the AS curve is vertical. If AD decreases at this time, prices will drop but GDP will tend to remain the same.

35. C: A person who has taken out a fixed-rate loan can benefit from inflation by paying back the loan with dollars that are less valuable than they were when the loan was taken out. In the other examples, inflation harms the individual or entity.

36. B: When AD for the goods produced by an industry decreases, one might expect the wages paid to workers in that industry to decrease as a result. However, because unions negotiate contracts with employers, wages of unionized workers tend not to fall in these circumstances. This tendency for wages to stay the same is known as "sticky wages."

37. D: Because the MPC is 0.9, the multiplier is 10 (1/0.1). Therefore, to attain an increase of $10 billion in AD, the government must increase spending by $1 billion ($1 billion × 10 = $10 billion).

38. B: The current account is a measurement of a country's net exports. If a country has a current account surplus, the value of the goods and services it is exporting is greater than the value of the goods and services it is importing.

39. C: The increased cost of gasoline increases the cost of transportation. This is a variable cost of supply, and so the aggregate supply curve shifts inward and upward. In the short run, aggregate demand would remain fixed, leading to a rise in prices and decreased GDP.

40. D: Opportunity cost is a measure of what a society gives up to produce a good (or goods). When the society decides to increase its production of Good X from 10 to 15 units, it gives up the ability to produce 4 units of Good Y (with production of Good Y dropping from 10 units to 6 units). The opportunity cost of the decision, then, is 4 units of Good Y.

41. C: GDP measures only the value of final goods and services provided in a nation. The value of inputs—such as aluminum or computer chips—is not included, nor is the value of illegally sold goods and services such as illicit drugs.

42. B: Any expenditure that will increase a firm's future productivity is considered investment. Of the items listed, only the construction of a new plant matches the definition.

43. D: Monetary policy is the practice of shrinking and growing the money supply in order to combat inflation or deflation and otherwise attempt to "adjust" the economy.

44. E: When demand for a foreign currency drops, the value of that currency drops. This makes it cheaper to buy goods from that foreign country.

45. D: In the long-run Phillips Curve, unemployment stays at the natural rate of unemployment (NRU). As a result, while price levels change increase and decrease, movement along the long-run Phillips Curve is only up or down.

46. C: Economists are interested in unemployment caused by changes in the business cycle. That is what cyclical unemployment measures. There will always be some measure of structural and frictional unemployment, and those are not typically considered when assessing the unemployment picture in a nation.

47. D: When the FOMC purchases bonds, that brings an increase to the money supply, and there is an increase in bond yields and bond interest rates. When the FOMC sells bonds, that decreases the money supply, and bond yields and bond interest rates go down.

48. E: Money can be used in trade and can make trade easier, but it is not necessary for trade, as people can barter for goods and services.

49. A: Cost-push inflation is caused when the price of a resource rises dramatically and unexpectedly. This is sometimes known as a "supply shock." A classic example is the supply shock experienced in the US during the 1970s when the price of oil dramatically increased.

50. E: According to the theory of rational expectations, people adjust their actions as a result of rational expectations of fiscal and monetary policy. The adjusted actions reduce the effects of the fiscal or monetary policy, and move the economy toward a natural rate of unemployment.

51. A: Economics is defined as the study of scarcity, the situation in which resources are limited and wants are unlimited.

52. B: A basic element of Adam Smith's thought is that, since economies have access to limited resources with which to produce services, they should specialize in producing those goods and services they can produce most efficiently.

53. A: The change in demand is 20% (1,000 − 800 = 200), and the change in price is 10% ($11 − $10 = $1). Because the change in demand is greater than the change in price, the demand is considered elastic. In this case, the price elasticity quotient is greater than 1.

54. C: Complementary goods or services are goods for which demand is linked. If demand for a good increases, the demand for the good's complement will also increase. It follows, then, that increased demand for Good A will lead to increased demand for Service B, which in turn will lead to increased revenue for the producers of Service B.

55. A: Consumer surplus is the area below the demand curve that is above the equilibrium price line, represented by Area A in this graph.

56. D: According to the Law of Diminishing Marginal Returns, marginal product will initially increase as the units of an input are increased, but then the curve will flatten out and eventually the marginal product will begin to decrease.

57. A: The marginal product of labor of the fifth worker hired is 2, the total output for 4 workers subtracted from the total output for 5 workers.

58. D: In the short run, a perfectly competitive firm should shut down if total costs exceed total revenue and if the total variable costs exceed total revenue. If total revenue exceeds total variable costs, the firm should continue production. The difference between total revenue and total fixed costs is not part of this determination.

59. E: Firms in a monopolistic competition are not efficient. They earn a profit above the minimum ATC, meaning they are not efficient productively, and they create output at a level less than the level of allocative efficiency.

60. D: The accounting profit is $220,000 − $200,000 = $20,000; the economic profit (or loss) is $220,000 − $200,000 − $40,000 = (−$20,000); and the opportunity cost of starting the new business equals $40,000 because that was the "opportunity cost" of the next-best forgone opportunity.

61. C: Statements A, B, D, and E are all correct. However, if the government imposes a tax on a good with a highly inelastic demand, producers can shift a lot of the cost of the tax onto consumers, since demand does not vary much as price increases.

62. C: The impact of a transaction on third parties not involved in the transaction is known as an externality. An externality can be positive, in which case it's a positive externality or social benefit. An externality can also be negative, in which case it's a negative externality or a social cost.

63. E: A market failure is any situation in which the production of a good or service is not efficient. In the cases listed, non-competitive markets allow for the underpayment of labor and the underproduction of a good or service; externalities are negative consequences assumed by parties not involved in a transaction; and public goods are an example of a good the market will not produce at all, or at efficient levels.

64. B: If the government establishes a price floor that is higher than the equilibrium price, supply will exceed demand, and there will be a surplus.

65. A: Perfect competition is a theoretical type of market more so than one actually found in real life. That's because it is the most efficient, operating where P = MR = MC.

66. B: If the firms in an oligopoly create a cartel, they will increase prices and lower productions when compared to the standards of a perfectly competitive firm in an attempt to increase profit.

67. E: By definition, I and II are correct: a public good is non-excludable and non-rivalrous. In addition, because users do not pay for public goods, it is difficult to determine how much a user values the good.

68. A: The long run average total cost curve of a firm is a curve that connects the minimums from all of the firm's different short run average total cost curves.

69. E: The opportunity cost of a producer's choice to produce one good is the loss of the ability to use the same resources to produce another good.

70. C: The marginal cost of each pizza is the cost to make that one additional pizza. In this case, the sixth pizza adds only $4 to the total cost, the lowest of all production levels given.

71. E: An increase in the supply of the hats and a decrease in demand would both cause the equilibrium price to decrease, not increase. If both supply and demand stayed the same, the equilibrium price would also stay the same. If government subsidies made it cheaper to produce the hats, the price would go down. If the supply of a substitute good went down, more consumers might be driven to buy the blue hats, causing demand to increase and the equilibrium price to increase with it.

72. C: The law of diminishing marginal utility states that at some point a consumer will notice less satisfaction from a good or service at each consecutive consumption level of that product.

73. A: The accounting profit equals revenues minus costs. Economic profit is also concerned with opportunity costs.

74. C: Because the PPF shows all the combinations of goods that can be produced with a given set of resources, it is bowed, signifying that some combinations of the two goods have different opportunity costs.

75. C: A labor union reduces the supply of labor, thereby raising the wage rate above the equilibrium wage rate that would be earned in a perfectly competitive labor market. The supply curve for labor shifts to the left when a labor market is unionized.

76. D: Firms are attracted by an economic profit, where MR is greater than MC, and will enter a market until a normal profit returns, where MR = MC.

77. E: A market that is monopolistically competitive is relatively easy to enter and exit and has high levels of competition. Therefore, firms will enter and exit the market if it is not in long-run equilibrium. When price/quantity is below the minimum of the average total cost curve firms will exit the market.

78. A: Taxes, subsidies, price ceilings, price floors, taxes, and government regulations can all be used to try to correct market failures, in which the market does not produce goods and services efficiently. Societies try to use some or all of these techniques to adjust the market's production of goods and services, including externalities of the goods and services.

79. B: The benefit to the company is known as a private benefit. The benefit to the neighborhood is known as the external benefit. Social benefits are the total of private benefits and external benefits.

80. C: A monopsonist faces an upward-sloping supply curve for labor, not a downward-sloping curve. The rest of the statements are all true.

81. D: If a society wants greater income equity, it will impose a progressive income tax, which taxes the wealthy at a higher rate; an inheritance tax, which prevents the wealthy from passing all their wealth on to the next generation; and a gift tax, which prevents the wealthy from simply giving their wealth away.

82. A: If a price ceiling is established, demand will increase. Supply, however, will decrease. A price floor must be placed at a price higher than the equilibrium price in order for it to have any effect on the market, and the government would not simultaneously institute a price ceiling and a price floor.

83. E: If demand for a firm's product is perfectly inelastic, consumers will buy the same amount no matter the price. Therefore, the demand curve will be a straight line traveling up and down on the graph. A price increase would lead to an increase in revenue, a price decrease would lead to a decrease in revenue, and no price change would affect demand.

84. C: Firms in perfect competition are price takers. Their MRP = [marginal physical product] × [price], and their demand curve is horizontal. Firms in monopolistic competition, however, face a downward-sloping demand curve: they must lower their prices to sell additional units.

85. D: It is true that scarcity causes producers (and other people) to make choices. Producers must choose what to produce with limited resources. It is also true that the choices a producer makes when faced with scarcity come with trade-offs. There are advantages and disadvantages to different production decisions. And, finally, calculating the opportunity cost of a choice provides a manner with which to measure the consequence of a choice and compare that against the consequence of other choices.

86. C: I, II, and III are correct. If a determinant of demand increases, demand will increase. That means that the demand curve will shift to the right, causing an increase in both the equilibrium price and the equilibrium quantity. An increase in a determinant of demand will not cause any movement to the supply curve.

87. E: Costs of a good borne by society include the cost to pay for the product ($100 in this case), known as the private cost; the indirect costs borne by society (unwanted pollution in this case), known as the external cost; and social costs, the total of private costs and external costs.

88. E: It is not true that if E_S is greater than 1, supply is inelastic. In fact, that is the definition of elastic supply. All the other options are true—a. is another way to define elastic supply, b. is true because the supplier has to sell the goods before they perish, c. is true because production processes are generally fixed in the short run, and d. is true because, given time, a producer can change supply.

89. C: Choice a. yields 50 utils, Choice b. yields 60 utils, Choice c. yields 63 utils, Choice d. yields 60 utils and Choice e. yields 34 utils. Since Kenny is maximizing utility, he should buy 4 of good X and 3 of good Y

90. E: The US federal government plays many roles in the US society. These include regulating industries, such as communication and food production; the imposition of taxes, such as the federal income tax; the provision of programs designed to help poor people who would otherwise suffer more, such as Medicare and Medicaid; and the provision of public goods, including the US military and the National Park system.

91. D: Because Jasmine's income will increase, she will be able to buy some increased combination of good A and good B, and her total utility will increase as a result.

92. C: In a perfectly competitive market, firms will operate where MR = MC.

93. D: Producer surplus is the area above the supply curve and below the equilibrium price line. If the equilibrium price decreases, the area between the supply curve (unchanged) and the price line (lowered) will be smaller – which means a decrease in producer surplus.

94. B: A monopolist produces at price above the minimum ATC, unlike a firm in perfect competition, and at an output below the intersection of the demand and marginal cost curves.

95. D: In the short run, Bob's should continue to operate even if total revenues are less than total costs provide total revenues are at least greater than total variable costs. This means that the variable costs of operating would be covered and at least some of the fixed costs would be covered. In Bob's case, however, total variable costs are not covered, and so Bob's should shut down instead of incurring greater expenses by continuing to operate.

96. D: By definition, a public good is one that is non-excludable and non-rivalrous. The non-excludable nature of a public good is stated by option D.

97. C: The firms in an oligopoly may collude intentionally or unintentionally. The rest of the options are wrong: an oligopoly has many barriers to entry, including great economies of scale. This creates a "kinked" demand curve. Because of the barriers to entry, an oligopoly has few firms, not many.

98. E: By definition, production in the short run is the time period during which a plant cannot increase production capacity, and production in the long run is the time period during which production capacity can be changed.

99. D: An economic system must decide what goods and services are produced, how they are produced, and who gets them. The economic system will not set supply or demand.

100. C: To determine the least-cost, profit-maximizing combination of inputs, the company should use both inputs to the point where their marginal revenue product is equal to their price.

How to Overcome Test Anxiety

Just the thought of taking a test is enough to make most people a little nervous. A test is an important event that can have a long-term impact on your future, so it's important to take it seriously and it's natural to feel anxious about performing well. But just because anxiety is normal, that doesn't mean that it's helpful in test taking, or that you should simply accept it as part of your life. Anxiety can have a variety of effects. These effects can be mild, like making you feel slightly nervous, or severe, like blocking your ability to focus or remember even a simple detail.

If you experience test anxiety—whether severe or mild—it's important to know how to beat it. To discover this, first you need to understand what causes test anxiety.

Causes of Test Anxiety

While we often think of anxiety as an uncontrollable emotional state, it can actually be caused by simple, practical things. One of the most common causes of test anxiety is that a person does not feel adequately prepared for their test. This feeling can be the result of many different issues such as poor study habits or lack of organization, but the most common culprit is time management. Starting to study too late, failing to organize your study time to cover all of the material, or being distracted while you study will mean that you're not well prepared for the test. This may lead to cramming the night before, which will cause you to be physically and mentally exhausted for the test. Poor time management also contributes to feelings of stress, fear, and hopelessness as you realize you are not well prepared but don't know what to do about it.

Other times, test anxiety is not related to your preparation for the test but comes from unresolved fear. This may be a past failure on a test, or poor performance on tests in general. It may come from comparing yourself to others who seem to be performing better or from the stress of living up to expectations. Anxiety may be driven by fears of the future—how failure on this test would affect your educational and career goals. These fears are often completely irrational, but they can still negatively impact your test performance.

Elements of Test Anxiety

As mentioned earlier, test anxiety is considered to be an emotional state, but it has physical and mental components as well. Sometimes you may not even realize that you are suffering from test anxiety until you notice the physical symptoms. These can include trembling hands, rapid heartbeat, sweating, nausea, and tense muscles. Extreme anxiety may lead to fainting or vomiting. Obviously, any of these symptoms can have a negative impact on testing. It is important to recognize them as soon as they begin to occur so that you can address the problem before it damages your performance.

The mental components of test anxiety include trouble focusing and inability to remember learned information. During a test, your mind is on high alert, which can help you recall information and stay focused for an extended period of time. However, anxiety interferes with your mind's natural processes, causing you to blank out, even on the questions you know well. The strain of testing during anxiety makes it difficult to stay focused, especially on a test that may take several hours. Extreme anxiety can take a huge mental toll, making it difficult not only to recall test information but even to understand the test questions or pull your thoughts together.

Effects of Test Anxiety

Test anxiety is like a disease—if left untreated, it will get progressively worse. Anxiety leads to poor performance, and this reinforces the feelings of fear and failure, which in turn lead to poor performances on subsequent tests. It can grow from a mild nervousness to a crippling condition. If allowed to progress, test anxiety can have a big impact on your schooling, and consequently on your future.

Test anxiety can spread to other parts of your life. Anxiety on tests can become anxiety in any stressful situation, and blanking on a test can turn into panicking in a job situation. But fortunately, you don't have to let anxiety rule your testing and determine your grades. There are a number of relatively simple steps you can take to move past anxiety and function normally on a test and in the rest of life.

Physical Steps for Beating Test Anxiety

While test anxiety is a serious problem, the good news is that it can be overcome. It doesn't have to control your ability to think and remember information. While it may take time, you can begin taking steps today to beat anxiety.

Just as your first hint that you may be struggling with anxiety comes from the physical symptoms, the first step to treating it is also physical. Rest is crucial for having a clear, strong mind. If you are tired, it is much easier to give in to anxiety. But if you establish good sleep habits, your body and mind will be ready to perform optimally, without the strain of exhaustion. Additionally, sleeping well helps you to retain information better, so you're more likely to recall the answers when you see the test questions.

Getting good sleep means more than going to bed on time. It's important to allow your brain time to relax. Take study breaks from time to time so it doesn't get overworked, and don't study right before bed. Take time to rest your mind before trying to rest your body, or you may find it difficult to fall asleep.

Along with sleep, other aspects of physical health are important in preparing for a test. Good nutrition is vital for good brain function. Sugary foods and drinks may give a burst of energy but this burst is followed by a crash, both physically and emotionally. Instead, fuel your body with protein and vitamin-rich foods.

Also, drink plenty of water. Dehydration can lead to headaches and exhaustion, especially if your brain is already under stress from the rigors of the test. Particularly if your test is a long one, drink water during the breaks. And if possible, take an energy-boosting snack to eat between sections.

Along with sleep and diet, a third important part of physical health is exercise. Maintaining a steady workout schedule is helpful, but even taking 5-minute study breaks to walk can help get your blood pumping faster and clear your head. Exercise also releases endorphins, which contribute to a positive feeling and can help combat test anxiety.

When you nurture your physical health, you are also contributing to your mental health. If your body is healthy, your mind is much more likely to be healthy as well. So take time to rest, nourish your body with healthy food and water, and get moving as much as possible. Taking these physical steps will make you stronger and more able to take the mental steps necessary to overcome test anxiety.

Mental Steps for Beating Test Anxiety

Working on the mental side of test anxiety can be more challenging, but as with the physical side, there are clear steps you can take to overcome it. As mentioned earlier, test anxiety often stems from lack of preparation, so the obvious solution is to prepare for the test. Effective studying may be the most important weapon you have for beating test anxiety, but you can and should employ several other mental tools to combat fear.

First, boost your confidence by reminding yourself of past success—tests or projects that you aced. If you're putting as much effort into preparing for this test as you did for those, there's no reason you should expect to fail here. Work hard to prepare; then trust your preparation.

Second, surround yourself with encouraging people. It can be helpful to find a study group, but be sure that the people you're around will encourage a positive attitude. If you spend time with others who are anxious or cynical, this will only contribute to your own anxiety. Look for others who are motivated to study hard from a desire to succeed, not from a fear of failure.

Third, reward yourself. A test is physically and mentally tiring, even without anxiety, and it can be helpful to have something to look forward to. Plan an activity following the test, regardless of the outcome, such as going to a movie or getting ice cream.

When you are taking the test, if you find yourself beginning to feel anxious, remind yourself that you know the material. Visualize successfully completing the test. Then take a few deep, relaxing breaths and return to it. Work through the questions carefully but with confidence, knowing that you are capable of succeeding.

Developing a healthy mental approach to test taking will also aid in other areas of life. Test anxiety affects more than just the actual test—it can be damaging to your mental health and even contribute to depression. It's important to beat test anxiety before it becomes a problem for more than testing.

Study Strategy

Being prepared for the test is necessary to combat anxiety, but what does being prepared look like? You may study for hours on end and still not feel prepared. What you need is a strategy for test prep. The next few pages outline our recommended steps to help you plan out and conquer the challenge of preparation.

Step 1: Scope Out the Test

Learn everything you can about the format (multiple choice, essay, etc.) and what will be on the test. Gather any study materials, course outlines, or sample exams that may be available. Not only will this help you to prepare, but knowing what to expect can help to alleviate test anxiety.

Step 2: Map Out the Material

Look through the textbook or study guide and make note of how many chapters or sections it has. Then divide these over the time you have. For example, if a book has 15 chapters and you have five days to study, you need to cover three chapters each day. Even better, if you have the time, leave an extra day at the end for overall review after you have gone through the material in depth.

If time is limited, you may need to prioritize the material. Look through it and make note of which sections you think you already have a good grasp on, and which need review. While you are studying, skim quickly through the familiar sections and take more time on the challenging parts.

Write out your plan so you don't get lost as you go. Having a written plan also helps you feel more in control of the study, so anxiety is less likely to arise from feeling overwhelmed at the amount to cover.

STEP 3: GATHER YOUR TOOLS

Decide what study method works best for you. Do you prefer to highlight in the book as you study and then go back over the highlighted portions? Or do you type out notes of the important information? Or is it helpful to make flashcards that you can carry with you? Assemble the pens, index cards, highlighters, post-it notes, and any other materials you may need so you won't be distracted by getting up to find things while you study.

If you're having a hard time retaining the information or organizing your notes, experiment with different methods. For example, try color-coding by subject with colored pens, highlighters, or post-it notes. If you learn better by hearing, try recording yourself reading your notes so you can listen while in the car, working out, or simply sitting at your desk. Ask a friend to quiz you from your flashcards, or try teaching someone the material to solidify it in your mind.

STEP 4: CREATE YOUR ENVIRONMENT

It's important to avoid distractions while you study. This includes both the obvious distractions like visitors and the subtle distractions like an uncomfortable chair (or a too-comfortable couch that makes you want to fall asleep). Set up the best study environment possible: good lighting and a comfortable work area. If background music helps you focus, you may want to turn it on, but otherwise keep the room quiet. If you are using a computer to take notes, be sure you don't have any other windows open, especially applications like social media, games, or anything else that could distract you. Silence your phone and turn off notifications. Be sure to keep water close by so you stay hydrated while you study (but avoid unhealthy drinks and snacks).

Also, take into account the best time of day to study. Are you freshest first thing in the morning? Try to set aside some time then to work through the material. Is your mind clearer in the afternoon or evening? Schedule your study session then. Another method is to study at the same time of day that you will take the test, so that your brain gets used to working on the material at that time and will be ready to focus at test time.

STEP 5: STUDY!

Once you have done all the study preparation, it's time to settle into the actual studying. Sit down, take a few moments to settle your mind so you can focus, and begin to follow your study plan. Don't give in to distractions or let yourself procrastinate. This is your time to prepare so you'll be ready to fearlessly approach the test. Make the most of the time and stay focused.

Of course, you don't want to burn out. If you study too long you may find that you're not retaining the information very well. Take regular study breaks. For example, taking five minutes out of every hour to walk briskly, breathing deeply and swinging your arms, can help your mind stay fresh.

As you get to the end of each chapter or section, it's a good idea to do a quick review. Remind yourself of what you learned and work on any difficult parts. When you feel that you've mastered the material, move on to the next part. At the end of your study session, briefly skim through your notes again.

But while review is helpful, cramming last minute is NOT. If at all possible, work ahead so that you won't need to fit all your study into the last day. Cramming overloads your brain with more information than it can process and retain, and your tired mind may struggle to recall even previously learned information when it is overwhelmed with last-minute study. Also, the urgent nature of cramming and the stress placed on your brain contribute to anxiety. You'll be more likely to go to the test feeling unprepared and having trouble thinking clearly.

So don't cram, and don't stay up late before the test, even just to review your notes at a leisurely pace. Your brain needs rest more than it needs to go over the information again. In fact, plan to finish your studies by noon or early afternoon the day before the test. Give your brain the rest of the day to relax or focus on other things, and get a good night's sleep. Then you will be fresh for the test and better able to recall what you've studied.

Step 6: Take a Practice Test

Many courses offer sample tests, either online or in the study materials. This is an excellent resource to check whether you have mastered the material, as well as to prepare for the test format and environment.

Check the test format ahead of time: the number of questions, the type (multiple choice, free response, etc.), and the time limit. Then create a plan for working through them. For example, if you have 30 minutes to take a 60-question test, your limit is 30 seconds per question. Spend less time on the questions you know well so that you can take more time on the difficult ones.

If you have time to take several practice tests, take the first one open book, with no time limit. Work through the questions at your own pace and make sure you fully understand them. Gradually work up to taking a test under test conditions: sit at a desk with all study materials put away and set a timer. Pace yourself to make sure you finish the test with time to spare and go back to check your answers if you have time.

After each test, check your answers. On the questions you missed, be sure you understand why you missed them. Did you misread the question (tests can use tricky wording)? Did you forget the information? Or was it something you hadn't learned? Go back and study any shaky areas that the practice tests reveal.

Taking these tests not only helps with your grade, but also aids in combating test anxiety. If you're already used to the test conditions, you're less likely to worry about it, and working through tests until you're scoring well gives you a confidence boost. Go through the practice tests until you feel comfortable, and then you can go into the test knowing that you're ready for it.

Test Tips

On test day, you should be confident, knowing that you've prepared well and are ready to answer the questions. But aside from preparation, there are several test day strategies you can employ to maximize your performance.

First, as stated before, get a good night's sleep the night before the test (and for several nights before that, if possible). Go into the test with a fresh, alert mind rather than staying up late to study.

Try not to change too much about your normal routine on the day of the test. It's important to eat a nutritious breakfast, but if you normally don't eat breakfast at all, consider eating just a protein bar. If you're a coffee drinker, go ahead and have your normal coffee. Just make sure you time it so that the caffeine doesn't wear off right in the middle of your test. Avoid sugary beverages, and drink enough water to stay hydrated but not so much that you need a restroom break 10 minutes into the test. If your test isn't first thing in the morning, consider going for a walk or doing a light workout before the test to get your blood flowing.

Allow yourself enough time to get ready, and leave for the test with plenty of time to spare so you won't have the anxiety of scrambling to arrive in time. Another reason to be early is to select a good seat. It's helpful to sit away from doors and windows, which can be distracting. Find a good seat, get out your supplies, and settle your mind before the test begins.

When the test begins, start by going over the instructions carefully, even if you already know what to expect. Make sure you avoid any careless mistakes by following the directions.

Then begin working through the questions, pacing yourself as you've practiced. If you're not sure on an answer, don't spend too much time on it, and don't let it shake your confidence. Either skip it and come back later, or eliminate as many wrong answers as possible and guess among the remaining ones. Don't dwell on these questions as you continue—put them out of your mind and focus on what lies ahead.

Be sure to read all of the answer choices, even if you're sure the first one is the right answer. Sometimes you'll find a better one if you keep reading. But don't second-guess yourself if you do immediately know the answer. Your gut instinct is usually right. Don't let test anxiety rob you of the information you know.

If you have time at the end of the test (and if the test format allows), go back and review your answers. Be cautious about changing any, since your first instinct tends to be correct, but make sure you didn't misread any of the questions or accidentally mark the wrong answer choice. Look over any you skipped and make an educated guess.

At the end, leave the test feeling confident. You've done your best, so don't waste time worrying about your performance or wishing you could change anything. Instead, celebrate the successful completion of this test. And finally, use this test to learn how to deal with anxiety even better next time.

Review Video: Test Anxiety
Visit mometrix.com/academy and enter code: 100340

Important Qualification

Not all anxiety is created equal. If your test anxiety is causing major issues in your life beyond the classroom or testing center, or if you are experiencing troubling physical symptoms related to your anxiety, it may be a sign of a serious physiological or psychological condition. If this sounds like your situation, we strongly encourage you to seek professional help.

Online Resources

Due to our efforts to try to keep this book to a manageable length, we've created a link that will give you access to all of your online resources:

mometrix.com/resources719/aepaeconomics

It's Your Moment, Let's Celebrate It!

Share your story @mometrixtestpreparation